THE COMPLETE
PATTERN BOOK
—FOR—
CAKES

LINDSAY JOHN BRADSHAW

MEREHURST

Published in 1993 by Merehurst Limited
Ferry House, 51-57 Lacy Road, Putney, London SW15 1PR

Copyright © Merehurst Limited 1993

ISBN 1 85391 351 0

A catalogue record for this book is available from the British Library.

Edited by Barbara Croxford
Designed by Christine Wood
Photography by David Gill
Typesetting by BMD Graphics, Hemel Hempstead
Printed by The Bath Press, England

CONTENTS

INTRODUCTION

Anyone who makes things, whether it is items of clothing to wear, household furnishings, or soft toys, will know that before work can commence, a pattern or template of some kind will be required to follow during each stage of production and ensure accuracy to create a neatly finished item. The same applies to cake decoration, from a simple 'Best Wishes' cake to the grandest of wedding cakes, you will always use a template, pattern or guide to assist in at least one and probably several stages of the decorative work. It may be that you only need to pin-prick a line as a guide on the cake side, or position a fancy board edge border, or make a runout figure to decorate a cake top. Whatever it is, good preparation, careful planning and execution of the work will be made all the more easier with the use of patterns.

The Complete Pattern Book for Cakes has been specially designed to meet the exacting requirements of the modern cake decorator, providing an extensive library of patterns, templates, layouts, stencil designs and reference in a large easy-to-use format, ideal for tracing or copying from. Simple explanations describe how to get the best results from the designs; however, the object of the book is to offer a wide and varied range of figures, faces, animals, motifs, hobbies, flowers, leaves and lettering, together with numerous complete arrangements, layouts and borders suitable for various occasions, celebrations and seasonal festivals. If you have already acquired a practical knowledge of various sugarcraft skills, this book will serve as an inspiration to further develop your creativity. Teachers and demonstrators will find it a useful source of practical teaching aids, in fact any sugarcrafter's bookshelf is incomplete without this invaluable companion. For those new to sugarcraft, use the simpler designs to get you started and as a reference to complement information you've gleaned from other specialist books covering various sugarcraft techniques or even to help with any tuition you may be receiving.

When the sugarcraft boom started a few years ago, cake decoration took on a new look with many different ideas in the creation and application of edible decor being introduced. Many of the so-called new techniques stemmed from existing methods from years ago, being adapted and improved upon by the many new talented and creative sugarcraft enthusiasts. Like any other popular craft, sugarcraft has and indeed still is being researched and developed, and as a result numerous improved edible cake coverings and modelling pastes, items of equipment, special pastes colourings and ingredients have become available. The fact that almost all the patterns featured in this book are interchangeable means that you can take advantage of those materials and tools, so don't just think of each pattern as only being suitable for execution in one medium or one sugarcraft technique, most of the designs have more than one application and several have many. For example the lettering alone can be produced in piping jelly, chocolate, cream, marzipan, sugarpaste or royal icing; the figures and animals can take on varying effects by experimenting with techniques such as stencilling, tube embroidery, brush embroidery, painting, appliqué, bas relief moulding, modelling and airbrushing.

Apart from the many basic and advanced techniques, and the various mediums that can be used to execute the patterns in a truly hand crafted fashion, you can also adapt some of the ideas to use in conjunction with commercially available cake decorations such as silver and gold horseshoes, ready-made hearts and bells. When it comes to flowers, the stem arrangements can be integrated with edible wafer flowers, good quality plastic flowers, even silk or fabric blooms – so even if you've never decorated a cake before there's no excuse for not having a go!

Good design is often a neglected area of cake decoration mainly because many people are afraid to try creating a layout or motif, or have tried, not succeeded and given up. If that is the case then this book should put an end to your problems. You can select everything for each individual cake from a motif, centrepiece, side design, board edging and suitable inscription, all ready drawn for you to copy, trace, reduce or enlarge accordingly. You can even cover the required page with waxed paper and pipe away!

When compiling the book from my own collection of patterns saved over the years, I have specifically selected a variety of styles to appeal to differing tastes. There is something for everyone, young and old, modern and traditional, easy and advanced, simple and intricate. Each pattern has been tried and tested so that you can benefit instantly from my experience. It is hoped that the contents of this book will provide endless hours of pleasure, but more importantly that it will be an encouragement to all sugarcraft artists to acquire more creativity and introduce a wider range of skills to their cake decoration. While the book reflects the current interest in patterns and templates by sugarcraft artists, inspiration will no doubt be found by embroiderers, designers, poster writers and flower arrangers, and will appeal to them also as an invaluable source of reference.

Lindsay John Bradshaw

USING THE PATTERNS

The format of this book enables you to lay the pages flat to make copying and tracing easier. You can even pipe straight from the book by placing waxed paper over the required pattern.

The size of the pages makes it possible to include full-size patterns for large wedding or celebration cakes, with a selection of side designs and other decorations.

If fancy or unusual cutters are unobtainable in your area, templates can be used instead. Templates can also be placed on sugarpaste or royal-iced cakes to outline or pipe linework around. Other uses include piping outlines ready for runout, piping jelly or brush embroidery work.

TRANSFERRING THE DESIGN

To re-create the design of your choice from the book, you will need to trace the image from the page. Using good quality tracing paper or greaseproof (waxed) paper, place the paper over the design and outline carefully and neatly including all the necessary detail. Use an HB pencil sharpened to a good clean point.

TRACING

To transfer the design onto paper for say a cake side template or onto card or oiled (parchment) paper for a reusable template, turn the tracing paper over and outline the design using an HB pencil again. Reverse the tracing paper once again and place into position on the paper. Finally outline with a slightly harder pencil, such as a 2H, to give a crisp line. Cut out the card template.

To transfer the design onto a cake, use the pin-prick method described below.

PIN-PRICKING

Trace the design of your choice from the page as described above. Instead of reversing the tracing to re-outline it, place the tracing on the iced surface taking care not to smear any unsightly pencil marks. Secure the tracing temporarily if required with a small piece of masking tape. Now simply follow the design with a fine pointed tool, mapping pen or similar implement to transfer a dotted image onto the icing. Make the dots as close or distant as you require to make a recognizable outline. Do not, however, press into the icing too much as this could result in large holes which may prove difficult to disguise.

OBTAINING THE CORRECT PATTERN SIZE

Having chosen the pattern, the next step is to ensure that it will fit comfortably into the available space on your cake. Even though many of the patterns in this book are shown in various sizes, sometimes an even larger or smaller size of a particular design may be required. You may also have figures that you have used previously for another cake which you wish to reduce or enlarge, or you may have seen a figure you would like to use but it does not fit your cake. Here are a few solutions to this problem.

The easiest answer would be to take the drawing to your local print-shop and ask for the image to be reduced or enlarged on their photocopying machine. If you intend to do this, it is a good idea to outline the actual figure with a fine black felt-tip pen before it is photocopied as the reproduction will then be much clearer.

Another suggestion is to invest in a pantograph. This implement, usually made from plastic, unfolds for use in reducing or enlarging drawings. A pointer follows the outline of the original drawing, while a pencil on the other end of the pantograph transfers the reduced or enlarged image.

For the majority of people, the most readily available method of reducing or enlarging drawings is the grid system, which is a reasonably simple way of changing the size and still keeping it in proportion. Draw a grid of squares in pencil over the relevant design (fig X); an average-sized greeting card can be divided into 18mm (¾in) squares. Then draw a second grid on another sheet of paper with larger or smaller squares, calculating these as closely as possible to fractions of the squares in the original grid.

The squares of both grids are numbered and lettered identically for easy cross-reference during the copying process. Follow the outlines from the original and copy them carefully on to the prepared grid. Using the squares as guidelines, you can copy, for example, the tip of the broom and the snowman's shoulder from the B4 square and so on until the picture is complete.

fig X

STENCILLING

MAKING A STENCIL FROM DESIGNS IN THE BOOK

SELECTING A DESIGN

There are stencil designs throughout the book for you to choose from covering all occasions and celebrations. All you need to do is select a design and make an accurate tracing of it onto tracing paper.

CHOICE OF STENCIL MATERIAL

There are a number of suitable materials for the production of stencils, some more widely available and some more reasonably priced than others.

Card The most readily available and the least expensive material is a firm card – that which is about the thickness of a cake or cereal box would be ideal. Although easy to cut, card has a short working life as it absorbs moisture from the food colourings and icings applied through it onto the cake. A new stencil would have to be made once the edges lose their definition.

Stencil card Most good art shops stock stencil card which is available in a light cream colour and a darker tan colour, both produce quality stencils. Stencil card is both easy to cut and waterproof. Stencils made from this card can be washed after use in warm water and, provided they are dried and then stored flat, they can be used on numerous occasions before the image definition shows any sign of deterioration.

Plastic Thin plastic or acetate is more durable than stencil card and should not deteriorate in any way providing it is washed and dried after use. Various gauges of plastic are available. For cake decoration, select a fairly thin gauge so as to achieve fine, delicate work on your sugarcraft creations. Plastic is a good flexible material which is ideal for use against a slightly uneven iced cake surface. It is available in good art stores or may be ordered on request.

Metal Thin gauge, food quality, stainless steel is the best type of metal to choose, but to cut the shapes you would need to take the design to a metal engineering company who would produce a professional quality stencil. Do check the cost first as this type of work is expensive. Many commercial stencils are produced in this manner and with care should last a lifetime. The main disadvantage with a rigid, metal stencil is that there is little flexibility and when using the stencil against an iced cake the surface must be perfectly flat to achieve precise results. This book presumes the use of thin gauge plastic or card stencils.

CUTTING A STENCIL

This is the most time consuming part of any stencil work, but it is essential to make a neat job of the cutting as the final design reflects the quality of the image on the stencil.

Transfer the tracing of the design onto the material of your choice. The rules around the designs in the book illustrate the overall area of the stencil material required to allow for both positioning on the cake and for material to hold onto while stencilling.

Place the material onto a cutting board (not the kitchen worktop) and, using a sharp craft knife, carefully and neatly cut out the stencil. Apply firm pressure on the craft knife to ensure a good clean cut. Take extreme care when cutting areas of the design where the lines are close together as one small slip of the knife can spoil the stencil. If you should cut a wrong line or slip with the knife, place a piece of thin adhesive tape over the back of the stencil and re-cut the area to remove excess tape. The repaired area will not last as long as the good parts of the stencil, but will enable you to use the stencil a few times.

Do not use scissors to cut out stencils, it is impossible to achieve accurate results with them. Craft knives are available in art or craft shops.

SELECTING STENCILLING MEDIUM

Surface	Stencil Medium
Royal icing or Sugarpaste	Royal icing Food colour (applied using an airbrush) Food colour (stippled using a short bristled paint brush)
Chocolate	Royal icing Buttercream
Fondant	Royal icing Buttercream Food colour (stippled or airbrushed)
Undecorated sponge cake	Sifted icing (confectioner's) sugar (white or coloured with edible petal dust powder) Cocoa powder

STENCILLING DIRECTLY ONTO ICED CAKE SURFACES

The following instructions are used when stencilling directly onto an iced cake surface:

Stencils are applied to iced cake surfaces the same way as described for prefabricated decorations except that instead of stencilling onto waxed paper or plastic wrap, the stencilling is applied directly onto the cake surface.

Extreme care must be taken when working on a finished cake surface not to get greasy or dirty finger marks transferred, always keep your hands and work area spotlessly clean.

Some cake surfaces may be too soft or the cake beneath too spongy to allow you to put pressure on the stencil to hold it firmly in position during stencilling. When working on royal-iced or sugarpasted cakes, secure the stencil with small pieces of masking tape. For chocolate surfaces keep the stencil in position with small weights placed on the corners of the stencils. Buttercream cakes need freezing to firm the cream and all materials prepared so that the cake can be removed from the freezer and decorated immediately before the cream starts to soften.

CREATING EFFECTS

The following guidelines are set out to help you get the maximum use from the stencil designs in the book. There are numerous ways to achieve interesting special effects but you should start with something easy and fairly simple. Once you have mastered the various methods of application you can go on to create new and original designs and experiment with challenging combinations of colour, texture and form.

SINGLE COLOUR APPLICATION

This is the easiest and quickest way to apply a stencil motif, simply use one colour spread across the whole stencil. Many of the designs in the book look most attractive stencilled in a single colour and often simplicity creates the most stunning effects.

WHITE ICING AND FOOD COLOURINGS

A multi-coloured image can be achieved quickly and simply by stencilling in white royal icing and allowing to dry completely. When dry, paint the icing with various edible food colourings as you would paint a plaque, filling in the detail and, if required, the shading and highlights. Eyecatching effects are created in this way and these are made more interesting by the raised effect of the stencilled icing.

MULTI-COLOURED STENCILLING USING MASKING TECHNIQUES

This is the most advanced and obviously the most time consuming method to use, however, it does create stunning coloured features for your sugarcraft creations. Good preparation is essential, plan in advance which colours are to be used and in what order each colour is to be applied.

Prepare the stencil as previously described and prepare the various coloured royal icings, creams or liquid food colourings (liquid or diluted paste colours if using the airbrush method).

Position the stencil on the cake top or side, securing as described with masking tape or small weights. Decide on the sequence in which the colours are to be applied and mask off any areas of the stencil that are not to be coloured at this stage. Masking is done by cutting small pieces of masking tape to cover the various cut-out shapes or by laying small pieces of thin card over the shapes and securing with a small weight. If using the airbrush method, any exposed iced surface should be masked or covered with greaseproof or waxed paper to prevent unwanted colour droplets or mist settling on the surface.

Apply the icing, cream or food colour (in the case of sprayed colour allow to dry a little) then remove the next portion of masking to reveal the cut-out area to be stencilled next, remembering to cover up cut-out areas already coloured, if required. Continue until all the cut-outs have received colour and the image is complete, carefully remove the stencil. Extra detail, painting or piped features may be added to further enhance the design.

CLEANING AND MAINTENANCE OF STENCILS

When stencils are used by cake decorators for sugar or food colour stencilling they can be subjected to frequent washing in cold water. It is important to care for your stencils and store them correctly after use ready for the next time.

Card These may only be wiped clean between stencil operations and then discarded. Cut a new stencil each time as washing after use will render the card unsuitable for accurate stencil work.

Stencil card After each use, place the stencil in the sink under cold or lukewarm running water and allow the water to flow over the stencil until no traces of icing or food colour remain. Remove from the sink and hold for a few seconds to allow most of the excess water to drain away. Then place the stencil flat on a clean tea towel laid on the work surface and allow to dry fully. Store flat ready for use again.

Plastic These may be submerged in warm water until the icing or colour is fully removed from the stencil. Dry the stencil with a clean tea towel taking care not to damage any intricate cut-out shapes. Store the stencils flat.

Metal Wash as for the plastic stencils, although hot water may be used. Allow the excess water to drain off the stencil and then carefully dry with a cloth. Take care not to damage or snag the intricate parts of the stencil with the cloth when drying. Place the stencils back in their original packing.

USING THE PREPARED STENCIL

FOR DIRECT STENCILLING AND BUILT-UP DECORATIONS
(Instructions for use with designs on page 67)

For direct stencilling or to make built-up icing decorations such as heart shapes, bell shapes, butterfly wings, flower petals and waterlily type decorations use the following method:

1 Place the prepared stencil onto waxed paper or plastic wrap – using plastic wrap gives a shiny surface to the royal icing. Ensure that the stencil cut-outs are in exactly the right position over the waxed paper.

For direct stencilling, position the prepared stencil onto the iced cake.

2 With your forefinger and thumb, hold the stencil firmly on the surface. Do not allow the waxed paper to move during the stencilling operation.

For direct stencilling, secure with masking tape or weights.

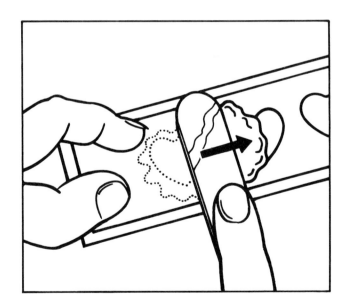

3 Using a palette knife, spread a small amount of royal icing across the stencil taking care to cover all the required area. Spread the icing away from the end held by your forefinger and thumb, spreading in the opposite direction would cause the stencil to lift and buckle.

4 To remove the stencil, hold the waxed paper firmly without disturbing the stencil (movement could distort the shapes). Then, gently lift and peel off the stencil starting at the end opposite to that being held. If you have difficulty lifting the stencil, use the blade of a small knife to ease it.
5 Prefabricated pieces should be dried under a gentle heat such as a desk or anglepoise lamp as for runout work. The stencilled sections will dry quickly and can be removed from their waxed paper backing ready for use. See page 67 for details of how to assemble the shapes.

CHILDREN'S DECORATIONS

Decorating a cake for a child is great fun. Here are a host of amusing designs to suit children of all ages. Bring a smile to a child's face by decorating a cake using a motif of their favourite toy or these delightful flower faces. Older children may like a popular sport or hobby depicted on their special cake. Colourful clowns and animals are always a good choice.

FLOWER FACES

These fun flower ideas are suitable for more than one sugarcraft technique and various edible media.

FUN ANIMALS

These examples are suited to runout work, marzipan appliqué, bas-relief and even outlining with piping chocolate and flooding with coloured icing or piping jelly. Have fun!

CHILDREN'S STENCILS

Children will adore these fun ideas stencilled in bright colours on the top of their birthday cakes.

These novelty faces make a jolly centrepiece for a party cake.

TOY BOX STENCILS

These popular toy box items make colourful decorations for a child's cake.

Birds, Butterflies and Animals

All kinds of birds and delicate butterflies make attractive cake designs for a range of
celebration cakes, especially weddings, anniversaries and engagements.
Animal designs are excellent for novelty cakes; children adore them too
(see also page 16), especially if their favourite pet is featured.

Swans and birds

BUTTERFLIES

Piped butterflies are usually associated with wedding cakes, although they are now also quite popular for anniversary, birthday and engagement cakes used in conjunction with a spray of sugarpaste or silk flowers. The four graduated sizes enable you to decorate multi-tiered cakes of varying diameters.
Styles A and B are most suited to outlining in royal icing or chocolate. Style D would look nice as a runout. Styles C and F are ideal for use as a stencil.
For all the butterflies, first make the wings and leave them to dry. Then make a card former, shaping a 'V' as shown. Line the former with a strip of waxed paper and using a No 1 or No 2 tube (tip), depending upon the size of the butterfly, pipe a body into the join, insert the wings and two stamens for antennae.

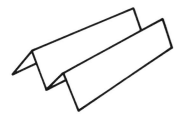

Size 1

Size 2

F

A

B

C

D

E

As seen
on the cover

Size 4

A

B

C

D

E

F

Size 3

A

B

C

D

E

F

31

BIRTHDAYS AND ANNIVERSARIES

Here are a few examples of cake top designs for birthdays and anniversaries.
Of course, the book is full of ideas for these occasions, especially in the Flowers section.
In Lettering you can choose your style of inscription to suit the cake design for that
perfect finishing touch.

Have a Jolly

Birthday!

Jane

Happy Birthday Twins

Bethan & Anna

Happy Anniversary

Happy

Anniversary

25yrs

CHRISTMAS

The rich traditional colours associated with this festive time of year give the sugarcraft
artist much scope for creating spectacular effects on their cake creations.
Use green, reds and browns in conjunction with the metallic colours of silver and gold to
accomplish the perfect Christmas look. The garlands and wreaths, jolly motifs and
delightful stencils included will fill you with inspiration.

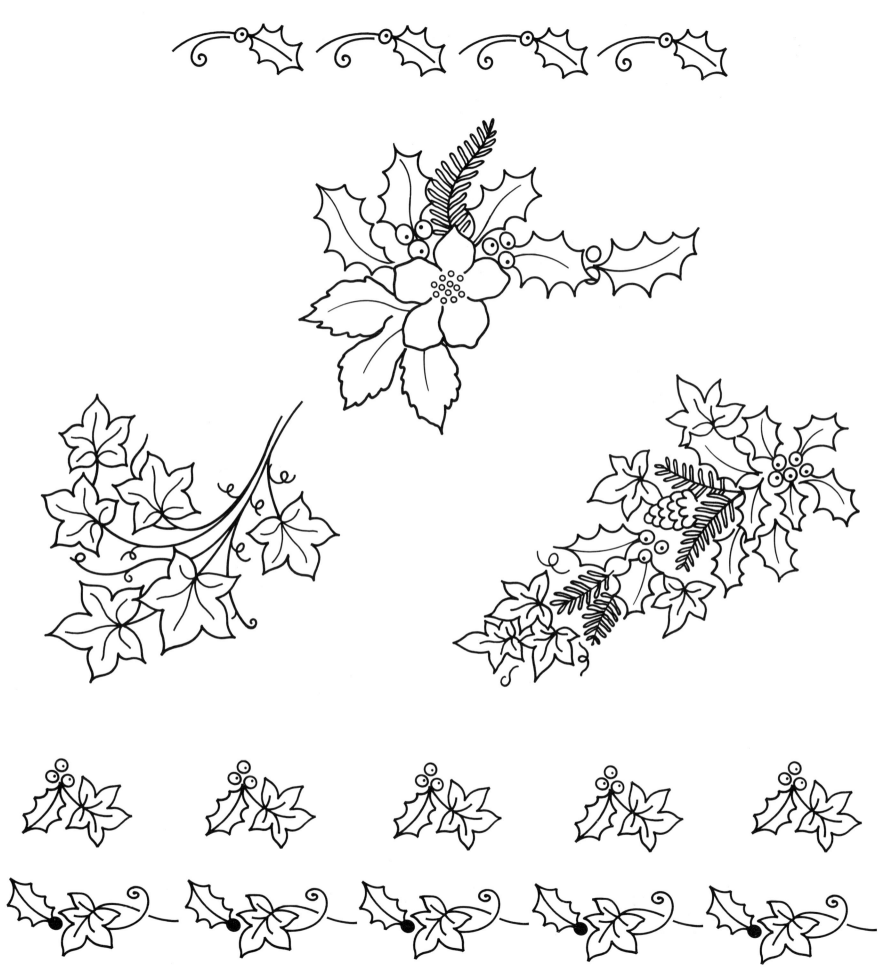

GARLANDS AND WREATHS

These garlands and wreaths could be used to form the main decoration of a cake, or reduced in size for the sides of a cake. They lend themselves to several forms of edible media and could be reproduced flat or in half relief.

CHRISTMAS MOTIFS

These festive motifs enable the sugarcraft artist to decorate Christmas cakes either simply in cut-out marzipan and sugarpaste or more elaborately in runout work depending on the time available.

CAKE TOP STENCILS

Two complete cake top designs – a quick and easy way to decorate.

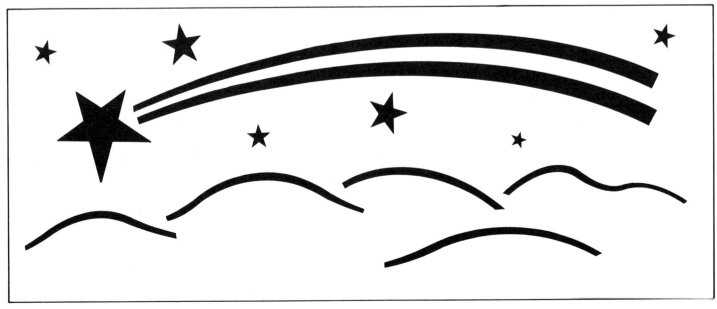

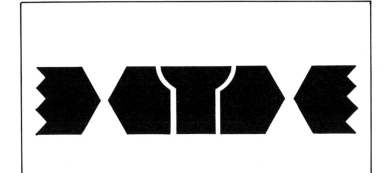

EASTER

Make a cake to say that spring has arrived! Daffodils, violets, catkins and pussy willow are all beautifully combined in various arrangements to provide a selection of designs suitable for Easter cakes and small fancy cakes. These flowers and the stencils overleaf are also ideal for Easter egg decoration.

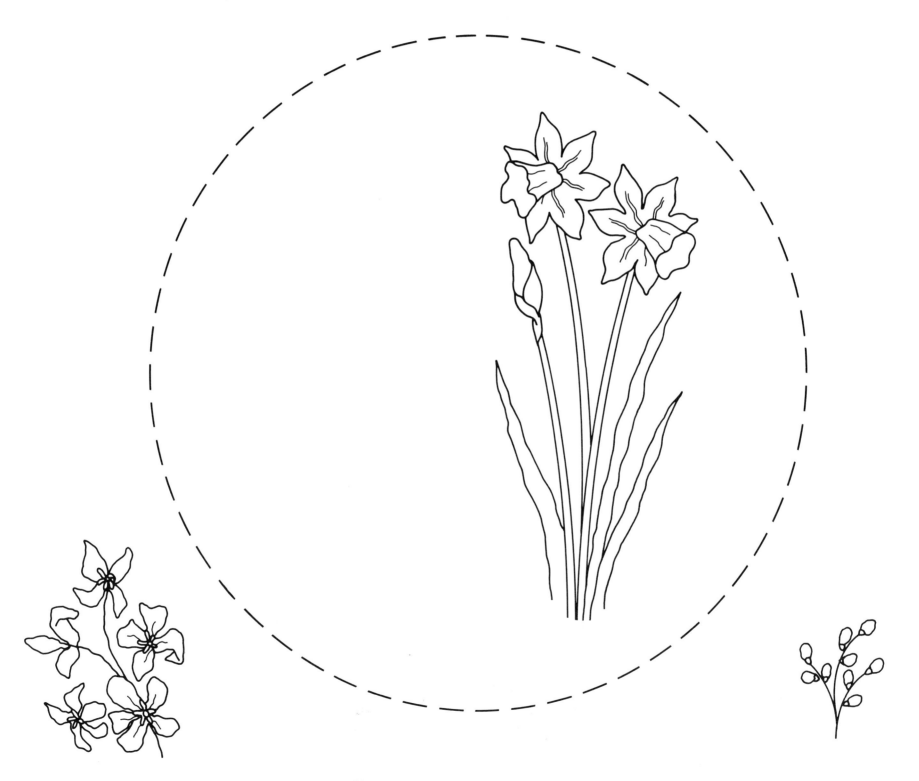

CAKE TOP DESIGNS

The ducks are ideally suited for cutting as a stencil
and applying directly to the cake top. Lettering,
linework and small bulbs complete the design.

VALENTINE'S DAY AND ENGAGEMENT

Flowers and engagements or Valentine's Day go hand-in-hand. Using the traditional heart shape as a basis for these designs, the selection covers ideas that can be accomplished in royal icing, marzipan, sugarpaste, chocolate and buttercream. The romantic effect required for engagement cakes can often be difficult to achieve. The designs provided here use complementary floral work to enhance traditional engagement motifs.

With Love

ENGAGEMENT FLOWERS

17.5 cm (7in) square cake top

17.5 cm (7in) diameter cake top

CAKE TOP DESIGNS

Make the figures as runouts or paint them directly on to the cake top. Directly piped lettering and a few small cut-out hearts make an attractive engagement cake or, by using the alternative lettering provided, a Valentine cake.

MOTHER'S DAY

Although fresh flowers are the traditional gift usually associated with this special day,
a cake with edible flowers would make an equally perfect tribute.
Choose from this selection of both traditional and modern designs, each suitable for more
than one sugarcraft technique.

WEDDINGS

The varied selection of beautiful flower and leaf motifs in this section provide endless scope for the all-important wedding cake decoration. All the popular flowers associated with weddings are featured together with the traditional heart and bell motifs. Many of the designs are shown in graduating sizes for use on multi-tiered cakes.

CAKE TOP DESIGN

Delicate butterfly and flower design for a single tier wedding cake.

Cake side template

20 cm (8in) diameter cake top

Piped line design

Delicate butterfly
Cut out the wing shapes from thinly rolled out modelling paste. Allow to dry, then paint the pattern detail on using edible food colouring with a fine paint brush. Pipe a body of royal icing, then attach the wings, supporting until dry (see also page 30).

Cake line

Cake board edge

WEDDING DESIGNS

These motifs can also be used as side 'fillers' on both sugarpaste-covered and royal-iced cakes.

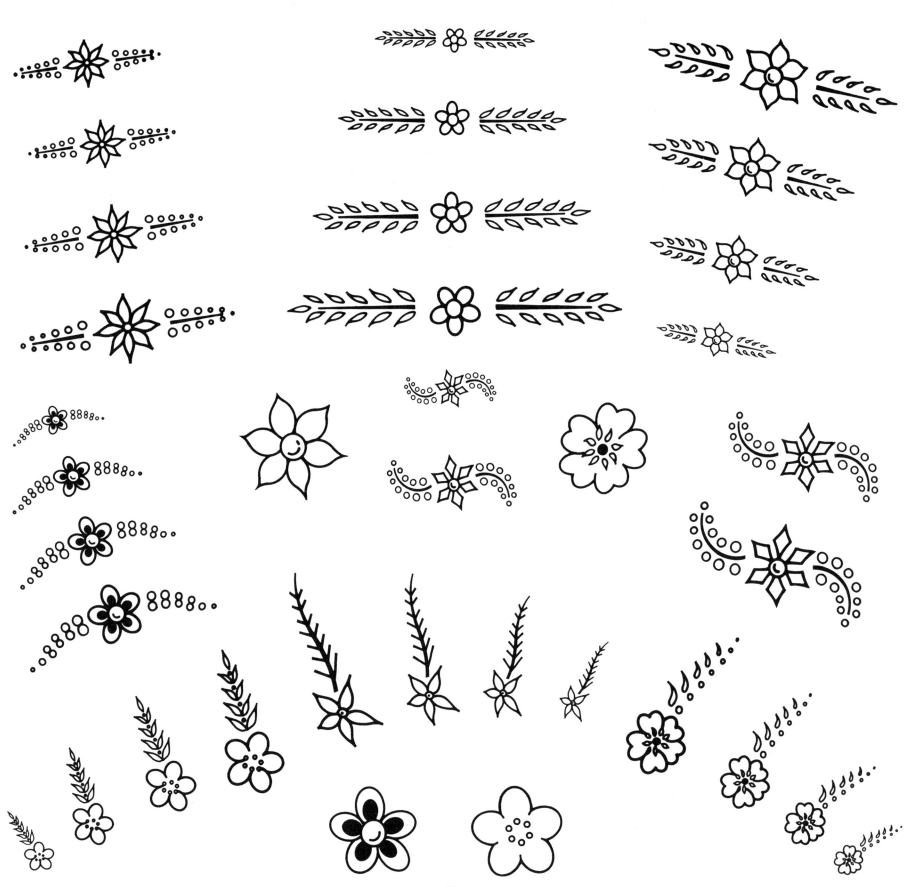

PREFABRICATED DECORATIONS

Bells, hearts, butterflies (see page 30) and flowers – use them as decorations on wedding cakes.

HEARTS AND BELLS

Hearts When dry use as required or decorate the edge with a line of royal icing piped using a No 1 tube (tip) (see page 11).
Bells When the stencilled bell shapes are completely dry, pipe two lines as shown using a No 1 or No 2 tube (tip).

Pipe the hammer for each bell onto waxed paper, allowing them to dry and then attaching them to the back of each bell shape with icing.

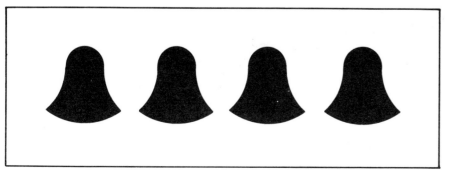

FLOWERS AND LEAVES

Pipe a bulb of stiff royal icing onto a small square of waxed paper, insert 4, 5 or 6 petals into the icing, overlapping each as you go. The petals may be inserted pointed end facing in or out to make various flower types. Allow to set, then pipe a contrasting coloured bulb for the flower centre. Edible petal dust, or airbrushed colour, will add attractive effects to the flowers.

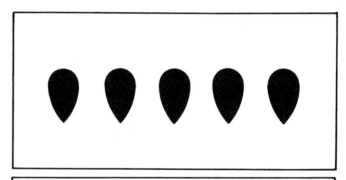

WEDDING SIDE PANEL DESIGNS

Side panels on wedding cakes will look most attractive with the inclusion of these dainty floral designs and rose sprays. The designs are provided in graduating sizes.

WEDDING FLOWERS

Magnolia, lily, freesia and dainty blossom are amongst the most popular wedding flowers.

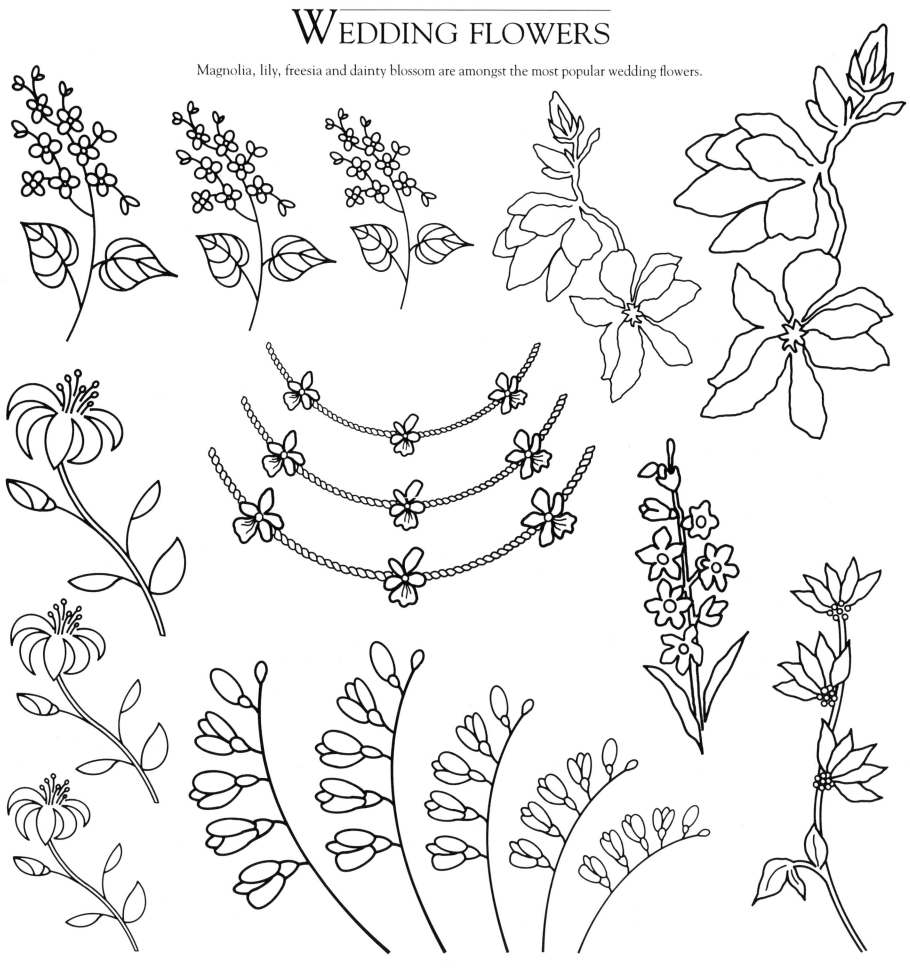

A wedding cake isn't complete without a few of these traditional motifs. The bells and hearts are shown in four sizes for use on multi-tiered cakes.

Size 1

Size 2

Size 3

Size 4

WEDDING STENCILS

Delicate and intricate wedding designs to decorate the sides or the iced cake board of a wedding cake.

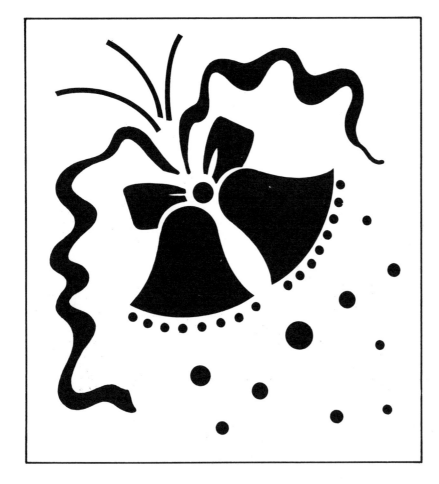

CHRISTENINGS

Traditional christening motifs combined with floral embellishments provide delicate designs which can be adapted for a boy or girl's christening cake. Simply make the design in an appropriate colour usually associated with this special occasion, namely blue for a boy, pink for a girl or lemon for either sex. Some of the figures and motifs overleaf would also be perfect for a baby's first birthday cake.

17.5 cm (7in) square cake top

FLOWERS

Hand-crafted flowers used by cake decorators can be made from royal icing, marzipan, sugarpaste, chocolate, buttercream and even rice paper. There are also a number of non-edible flowers which have become more and more popular, especially for commercial use, over the past years. They include fabric, silk, plastic and dried flowers – all widely available from a variety of outlets such as florists, craft shops and of course sugarcraft suppliers. Although non-edible flowers can be purchased and used to attractively decorate cakes, the aim of this section is to stimulate and inspire you to make and create flowers from various edible media using different sugarcraft methods and techniques, then to decoratively arrange them on your cake creations. Hand-crafted work is far more satisfying to the person working it and doubly satisfying when the cake can be given as a gift expressing a personal and caring touch.

Just follow a few simple guidelines as you use the individual themes of each page to provide single blooms, sprays, side designs, full cake tops and many more examples of floral work to suit cakes for every occasion.

SUGARCRAFT TECHNIQUES

A brief description of the more popular sugarcraft techniques suitable for flower making are described here.

PAINTING
The same techniques used for painting scenes, figures and animal motifs on cakes and plaques can be successfully used to paint very attractive floral pictures. Mix edible food colours, paste or liquid with an edible white confectioner's compound to make the paint. Outline the design of your choice, then use various tints and shades to produce life-like flowers and leaves.

CUT-OUT
This type of flower makes a quick and easy decoration for gâteaux and celebration cakes. It is also ideal for beginners to lead them into more advanced floral techniques.

FLOODWORK
A popular method of producing decoration for many types of cakes. The floodwork technique can be used for chocolate and piping jelly work as described on page 106.

ROYAL ICED FLOWERS

Piped full-relief A small square or circle of waxed paper on which to pipe the flower is placed on a flower nail. Using a special petal piping tube (tip), single petals can be piped in formation to create a full flower. The flowers can range from flat type flowers like primroses and violets through half-relief ones like daffodils with trumpets and sweet peas with overlapping petals, and even three-dimensional full flowers like roses. After drying, the flowers are peeled away from the waxed paper and used in arrangements. Attach the flowers to the cake top with tiny dabs of royal icing. The same technique can be used to make buttercream flowers (see page 108).

Piped half-relief Using tube (tip) Nos1 and 2, bulb, petal and teardrop shapes are piped in sequence to form full flowers. A small centre bulb completes the flower and represents the stamen. This type of flower may be piped on waxed paper to be used as required for decoration, or they can be piped directly onto a cake top, side or prepared plaque.

STENCILLING

A step-by-step method of this technique is provided on page 98. See also Stencilling on page 8.

BRUSH EMBROIDERY

A technique used predominantly for floral designs but equally useful for animal and figure work. A line of royal icing is piped to form an outline, which is then brushed inwards while still soft. An addition of clear piping-gel to the icing will delay the drying process, thus giving more time to work the design accurately.

TUBE EMBROIDERY

A method of reproducing various embroidery stitches in icing. Fine tubes (tips) are used with various appropriately coloured icing to pipe satin stitch, chain stitch, running stitch and many many more. Beautiful floral work can be accomplished using this technique. Pipe directly onto a sugarpaste, royal iced or chocolate surface.

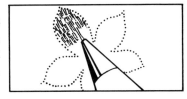

DESIGNING THE CIRCULAR FLOWER

To obtain a more consistent shape within the design of a flower, you can combine geometric principles and the techniques of tracing. Most open flowers can be based on a circle, if the circle is then divided into the number of petals required, each segment can be used to contain a drawing or outline of a single petal. To form an accurate flower drawing, repeat the petal shape in the remaining segments by tracing.

  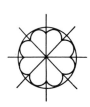

ARRANGING FLOWERS

Strict rules are not required when arranging flowers for cake decoration. An arrangement or layout that looks attractive and appeals to one person may look totally wrong to another. All that is necessary are a few simple guidelines to follow.

To spend too much time arranging and fixing, flowers can result in an arrangement that looks 'over worked', making an over-fussy and not too pleasing an effect. A simple, natural look is the one to aim for whether you want to produce a formal or informal look.

FORMAL ARRANGEMENTS

This type of arrangement will be governed to some extent by an imaginary outline shape, maybe a triangle, a crescent or an oval. Or the arrangement may take on a symmetrical design, being the same on both sides of a dividing line. Formal arrangements are useful for centring on a cake top or on a more 'fixed' type of overall cake design.

Formal

Informal

INFORMAL ARRANGEMENTS

Informal arrangements are more difficult to achieve than formal ones as there are no real rules to adhere to such as geometric principles. Therefore, the design takes on a more loose appearance with plenty of naturally flowing curved effects being allowed to take over. Having said this, informal does not mean untidy – spend as much time as you feel necessary to create a relaxed, total look to the finished work.

Informal arrangements are built up by eye appeal, by the sugarcraft artists appreciation of the materials being used, the positioning, and also the occasion for which the flowers are intended.

An equal number of flowers used in the arrangement.

All flowers arranged on same level or plane.

After arranging the stems, take care to position the flowers as naturally as possible, and not all on the same plane. This applies to both natural and imaginary flowers. To explain this, below are two flower arrangements, one with all the flowers on the same horizontal plane and the other more acceptable naturally arranged type of grouping, using varying levels or heights for each flower.

A more natural grouping is achieved by using an odd number of flowers.

Using similar curved stems but arranging the flowers on varying levels results in a more natural and informal appearance.

Using the same plane or level for each flower is sometimes inevitable on most segmented type cakes, such as a layer cake and large gâteau. An alternative method of arrangement would be to vary the flower levels on alternate segments.

Two design layout techniques widely used by the sugarcraft artist can be seen here used to display flowers as a decorative theme.

Design repetition
The same design in each division of a segmented layer cake.

Design alternation
Segmented layer cake with two alternating sectional designs.

MAKING A START

First try to visualize the effect you are trying to achieve – get ideas and inspiration from the complete designs and patterns featured in this book.

Unlike arranging fresh or dried flowers, you will probably have to create your own stem shapes for your 'designed' flowers rather than relying on the ready 'shaped' stems of fresh flowers. It is generally more difficult to achieve a natural flowing look with straight stems, so select curved and flowing type stems to begin with – straight stems create a more formal, rigid look. This, incidentally, is utilized quite considerably in cake decoration for some side designs, corners or where a real symmetrical look is required.

The form and arrangement of stems will sometimes be governed by the shape of the cake top and space available on it. A round or oval cake for instance will lend itself particularly well to curvy type groupings, whereas layer or bar cakes can carry straight stems easier – square cakes will accept both curved and straight. This is not a strict rule to adhere to, more a guide until experience is gained, as any shape of stem can be used on any shape of cake and still produce excellently balanced designs.

Generally it is better to use a limited range of flowers, rather than take one of each to produce your design, at least to begin with until you become more experienced at working with and combining varieties. The exception to this is if you are making a mixed posy, or collection of say summer blooms, where a wide range of colours and shapes is utilized.

PLANNING YOUR FLORAL DESIGN

Listed here are a few easy-to-follow guidelines to help you plan your design:

- Always take into account the type of surface on which the flowers are going to be used – royal icing, sugarpaste, chocolate, marzipan, buttercream etc.

- Give much consideration to the occasion for which the cake is intended, this will have enormous bearing on the selection of flowers. Is it a wedding, birthday, anniversary, man's cake etc?

- Assess the size of the cake – how big or small does the arrangement need to be?

- Decide upon your colour scheme for the background, ie the icing, sugarpaste or is it a dark brown chocolate covering?

- Select the type of flowers and determine the size required. Do you require flowers of an equal size or a mixture of small, medium and large.

- Select the background material, leaves and stems, and some foliage for the sides of the arrangement, ensuring that the stems curve the correct way for their position within the arrangement.

- When you have selected the flowers for the front of your arrangement, you may simply need a few fillers to complete the look.

- Use flowers of different heights so that the shorter ones can be used in front of the taller ones to hide the stems.

- Do not overcrowd arrangements, leave some space and 'air' between each flower and the leaves.

Designing and Making

Having taken into account the various elements that need to be considered in planning your floral design, give a little thought to the next stages of designing – Flower Colours, Leaves and Foliage.

FLOWER COLOURS

These range from the palest tints through to very strong and rich, deep colours. Flowers are natural colours and therefore are generally acceptable to the human eye. In this respect the sugarcraft artist needn't worry too much about possible lack of harmony when using vivid colours, except in extreme instance of combination – even then they can be successfully incorporated into a design. The reason being we accept these natural colours as belonging to the flowers themselves and not to the cake itself.

Bear in mind the occasion the cake is intended for, the sex of the recipient and any other factors that may govern choice of pale, pastel or deep flower colours, such as the colour of bridesmaids' dresses to be used on a wedding cake.

LEAVES AND FOLIAGE

These should be studied carefully before attempting to use them in floral decoration. There are long narrow leaves belonging to the daffodil, iris and tulip type flowers, then there are the oval leaves of rose and fuchsia, the former 'group' of leaves being without veins, the latter having veins.

Study also leaf edges which vary tremendously – the plain, some with serrated edges and also the deeply cut and divided types – not to mention the various outline shapes. Leaf joints to main stems should also be noted to make them look right. This awareness will result in near botanically perfect reproductions on your cakes – if that is what you are aiming for! Of course, many cake decorators are happy to produce a pleasing, colourful group of flowers on a cake without becoming involved with all the intricacies – create your own 'designer' flower and leaf ideas. There is lots of scope for imaginary flowers if you prefer – you won't be copying nature so you can afford to bend the rules a little!

Important Details

Here are a few helpful suggestions to ensure success with your arrangements:

- Use a selection of flowers in various stages of 'growth', such as tight buds, semi-open flowers, three-quarter open flowers and fully opened ones.

- Use flowers of different lengths and avoid placing flowers of the same height next to each other – have an up and down effect, rather than all the blooms on the same level or plane.

- Use flowers of different heights so that the shorter ones can be used in front of the taller ones to hide the stems.

- Group flowers in different shapes as a 'thread' running through an arrangement rather than all in one 'clump' with leaves as an unattractive 'collar' around them.

- After selecting your flowers and when arranging them, grade the flowers according to size and colour. Use the largest and darker coloured flowers towards the centre with the paler, smaller ones at the edges.

- All the stems should radiate from one central point, rather than positioned irregularly like a 'pin cushion'. Use curved flowing stems at the sides.

- Do not overcrowd arrangements, leave some space and 'air' between each flower and the leaves.

- The number of flowers used will be governed by the area of available space in proportion with the size of the cake top or side, the size of each individual flower and whether any other decoration is to be incorporated within the design, such as a name or inscription. Whatever the eventual total number of flowers is, a more natural appearance will be achieved by using the nearest odd number. Exceptions to this occur on equally numbered segmented gâteaux or layer cakes.

STEM LAYOUTS

These actual size stem pattern layouts are for 20cm (8in) cakes but they can easily be reduced or enlarged if necessary. Trace the pattern on to the cake and pipe with appropriately coloured icing. The reduced drawings will give you some idea of where to position the flowers.

ARRANGEMENTS

Achieving a pleasing balance of flowers, stems and leaves in an allocated space on differing shaped cakes can be quite daunting to a beginner. These examples give some ideas of how to create an attractive overall appearance. Use these as a basis for developing your ideas as you progress.

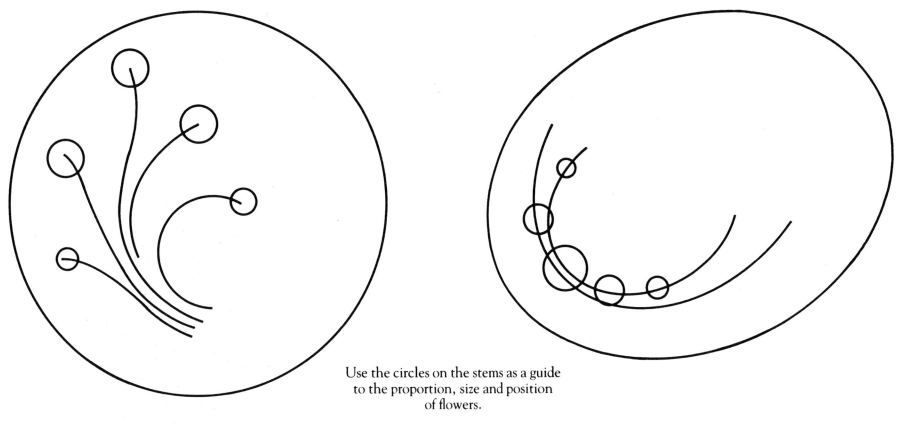

Use the circles on the stems as a guide
to the proportion, size and position
of flowers.

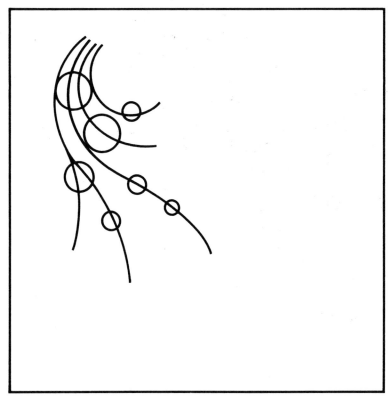

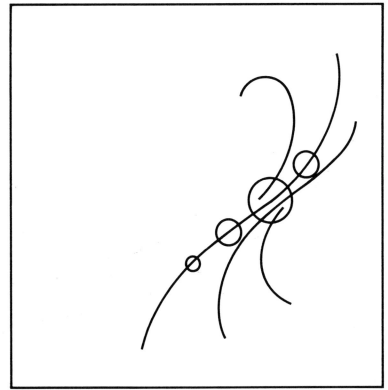

ORCHID

The beautiful orchid bloom is always associated as a wedding flower. A few attractive spray arrangements, together with a cake top and side design, provide much inspiration for the creative sugarcraft artist. Try orchids in brush embroidery – they are exquisite!

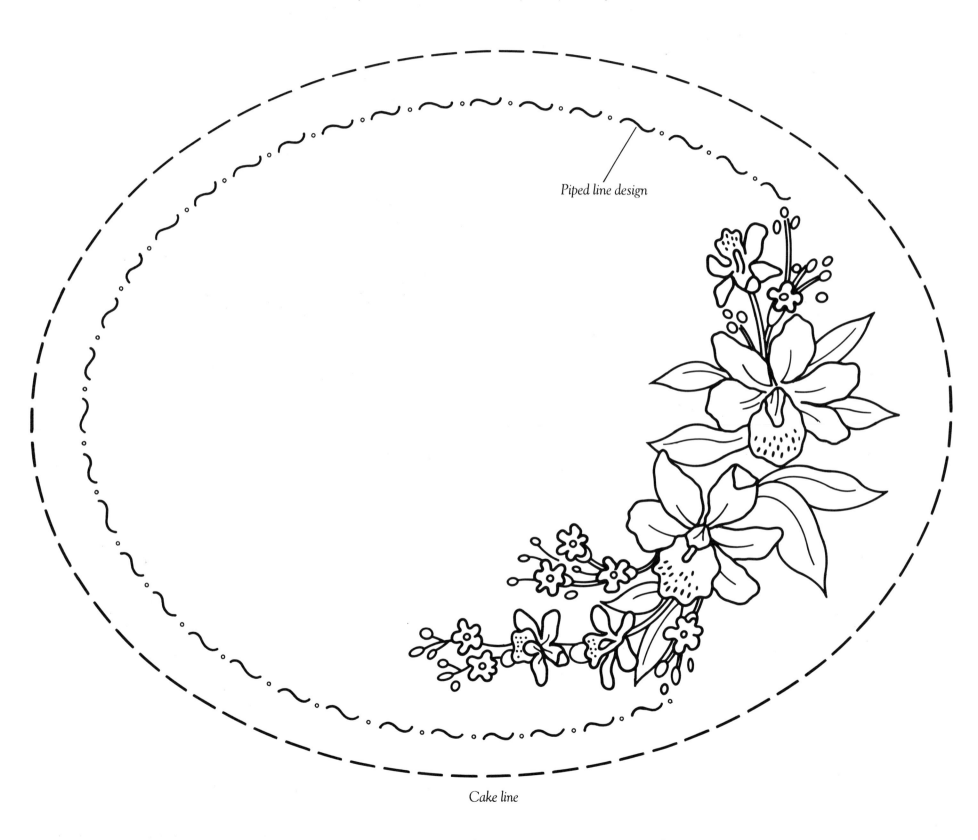

Piped line design

Cake line

Cake side template

- -

- -

ROSE

Probably the most well liked flower of all time, the rose in many various forms has long been associated with cake decoration. Suitable for making in numerous edible media, the rose will find a place on many of your sugarcraft creations.

Graduating sizes for multi-tiered cakes

Circular rose garland
for cake top

FUCHSIA

The beautiful fuchsia is somewhat neglected as a flower for cake decoration.
With the stunningly subtle colour combinations and 'lively' appearance of the blooms, fuchsias make an
ideal subject to enhance your cakes.

HOW TO MAKE A CUT-OUT FUCHSIA

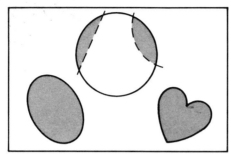

Prepare shapes as shown from thinly rolled out sugarpaste or marzipan in appropriate colours.

Assemble as shown directly onto the cake top or side, attaching together with water or a little royal icing.

Pipe the stamen as shown using royal icing with a fine tube (tip), such as a No 0 or 1.

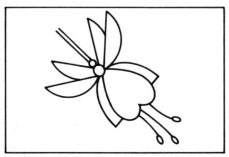

Complete the flower with the heart shape, then pipe on a thin stem using green-coloured royal icing.

HOW TO WORK A FUCHSIA

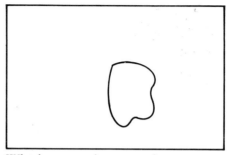

Whichever medium you choose to work in, always start with the basic shape of the petals (*corolla*).

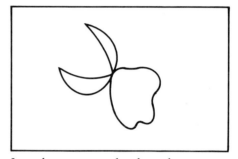

In order to create depth to the flower, the next stage is to work the distant sepals.

Using a fine tube (tip), pipe the stem (*pedical*), then add the foreground sepals and further work to complete the petals.

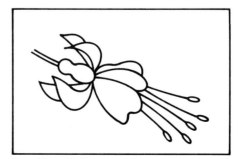

Finally add the ovary (stem joint) and pipe the stamen using a fine tube (tip), such as a No 0 or 1, in a suitable colour.

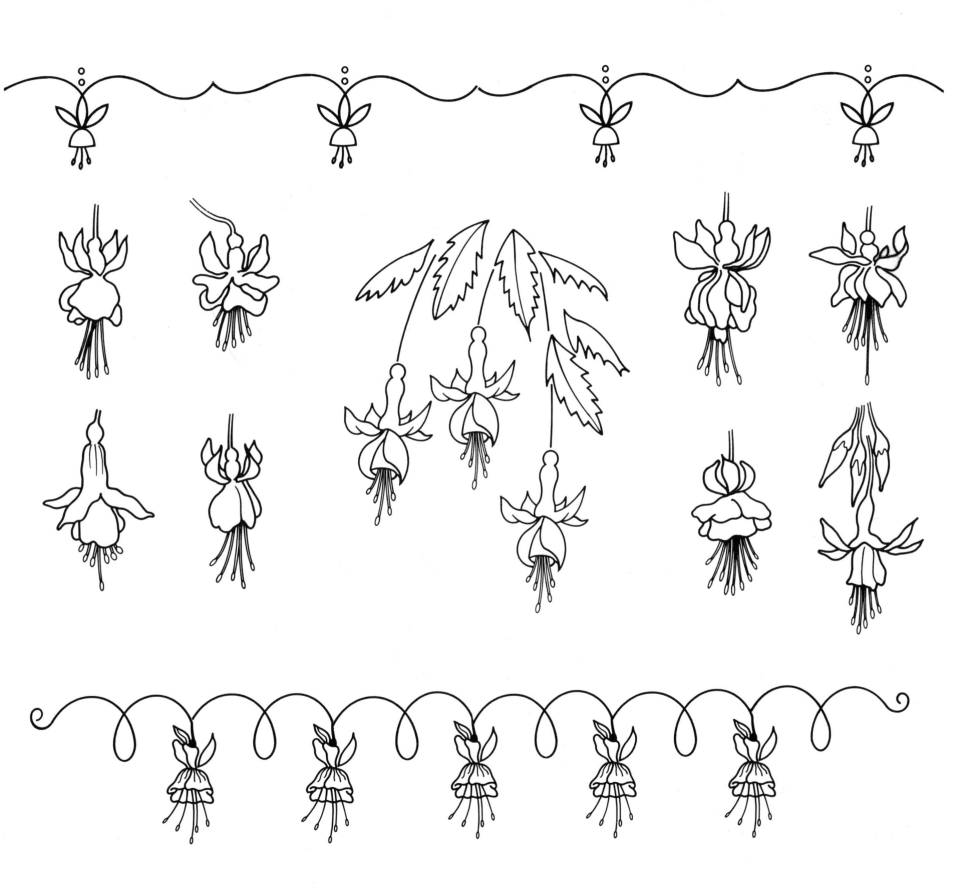

LILY OF THE VALLEY

This delicately beautiful miniature flower is usually associated with wedding cakes, but looks equally at home as a decoration on other special occasion cakes. Various sugarcraft techniques can be used for most of the designs shown here.

HOW TO PIPE LILY OF THE VALLEY

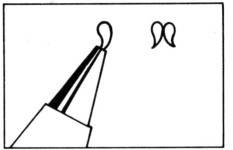

Method One
Use a fine piping tube (tip) with white royal icing or buttercream.

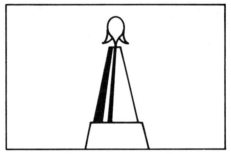

Over-pipe the two petals with a third larger pointed bulb shape to complete the flower.

Method Two
Pipe a bold bulb shape with a point on the end, using a No 1 tube (tip).

Using a finer tube (tip), pipe a curvy, scalloped-type line as shown for the petal edges.

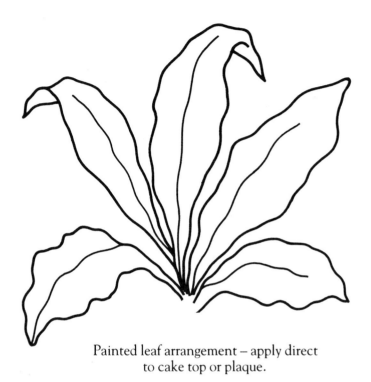

Painted leaf arrangement – apply direct to cake top or plaque.

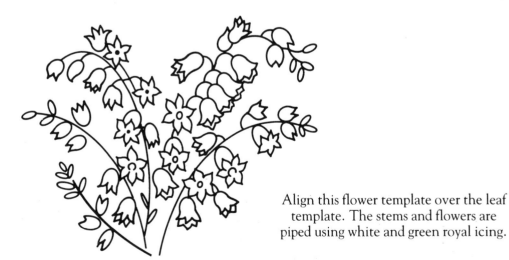

Align this flower template over the leaf template. The stems and flowers are piped using white and green royal icing.

See page 98 for a lily of the valley stencil design.

90

BRUSH EMBROIDERY

Brush embroidery is particularly effective for flowers but these templates can also be used for other sugarpaste techniques.

Violet

Cistus

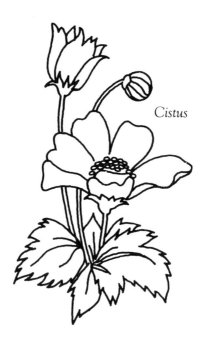

Daisy

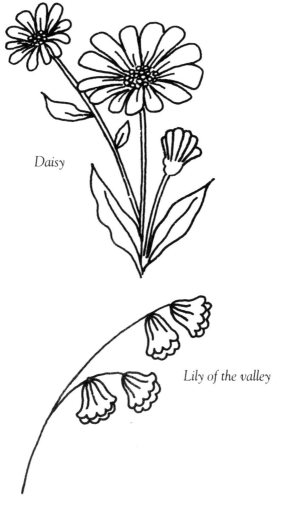

Lily of the valley

Poppy

Blackberry

Clover

Poinsettia

Rose

Fuchsia

Pansy

Fuchsia

Magnolia

Camellia

Daisy

Stems and fillers

Natural looking stem configurations can be difficult to achieve. Here is a useful selection of single and grouped stems, together with some 'fillers' with which to complete your arrangements.

LEAVES AND FOLIAGE

Here is a variety of leaves and foliage that can be accomplished using various sugarcraft techniques and materials. Use the leaves on their own or in conjunction with other designs in the section. For botanically correct designs, match the leaves to the correct flowers.

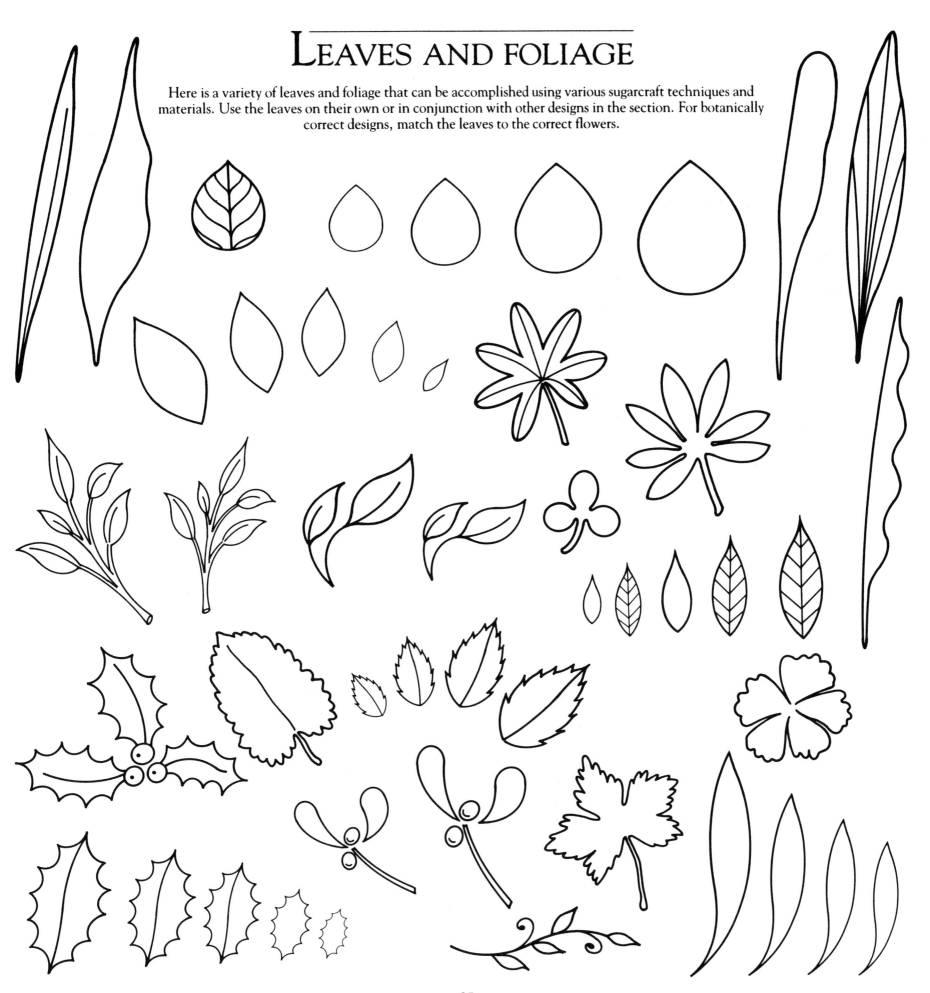

VASES AND BASKETS

An alternative to arranging flowers with just leaves and stems could be to present them in a decorative vase or basket. Many of the floral designs could be adapted for use with this varied selection of containers.

FLOWER STENCILS

Stencils provide a quick, easy and accurate method of applying designs to cake tops and sides. Here are a selection of floral designs ready for you to prepare a stencil from – as shown. The designs could also be stencilled onto prepared plaques (see page 160 for plaque shapes) which are then attached to a cake.

HOW TO STENCIL FLOWERS

Select your design, trace onto oiled stencil card or thin card and cut out using a sharp craft knife.

Using the first finger and thumb, hold the prepared stencil firmly in place on the cake top or plaque, or secure with masking tape.

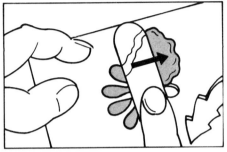

Spread coloured royal icing or buttercream over the cut-out parts using a small bladed palette knife, then remove the stencil.

Built-up flowers
Stencil petals onto waxed paper and allow to dry. Remove and assemble as shown. Pipe a centre bulb with royal icing to secure. (Petal shapes opposite.)

Petal shapes for built-up flowers

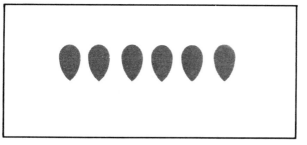

Use these shapes as leaves or petals to form flowers. For petals – the shapes above can be used with the pointed end in to the centre of the flower or facing outwards.

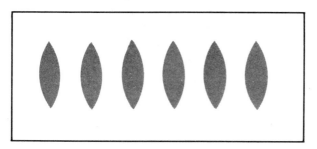

SINGLE BLOOM STENCILS

These stencils of single blooms look very effective in coloured icing on a cake top accompanied
by an inscription.

Alstroemeria

Allium

Petunia

Campanula

Poinsettia

Lavatera

Osteospermum

Rose

Potentilla

Dianthus

Fuchsia

Magnolia

FLOODWORK FLOWERS

A selection of outline designs ideal for runout icing floodwork techniques, but equally attractive when carried out in chocolate and coloured piping jelly. The designs are also suitable for other sugarcraft techniques.

HOW TO PIPE JELLY FLOODWORK FLOWERS

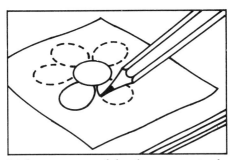

Make a tracing of the design required onto greaseproof (waxed) paper as described on page 6.

Place the tracing onto the sugarpaste-covered or royal-iced cake and pin-prick the outline onto the surface.

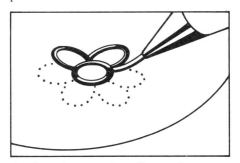

Outline the complete flower shape using a No 1 or No 2 tube (tip) with piping (thickened) chocolate.

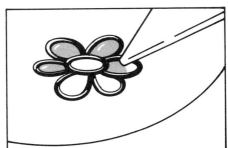

Using a small piping bag, flood-in the petals, centres and leaves with brightly coloured piping jelly.

Circular garland
for cake top

BUTTERCREAM FLOWERS

Buttercream flowers are quick and easy to make. Here are some examples of the more popular flowers using this versatile medium. Follow the step-by-step drawings as you pipe. Store them in the refrigerator until required.

HOW TO PIPE BUTTERCREAM FLOWERS

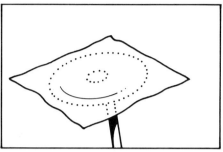

Prepare a flower (rose) nail for piping by attaching a small square or circle of waxed paper with a dab of buttercream.

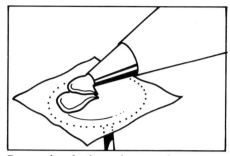

Pipe individual petals onto the paper, rotating the nail as you work. Use coloured buttercream and a petal tube (tip).

To create pointed petals, such as daffodils and narcissi, taper each petal to a point using a moistened fine paint brush.

Pipe a bulb of coloured buttercream in the centre, then pipe small dots or spikes to represent stamen, using a fine tube (tip).

HOW TO PIPE BUTTERCREAM LEAVES

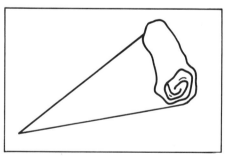

Bought leaf tubes (tips) can be used. To make a leaf piping bag, fill a paper piping bag with green buttercream.

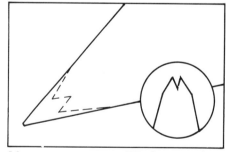

Using scissors, cut a 'W' shape at the point of the bag. The further away from the point you cut, the wider the leaves.

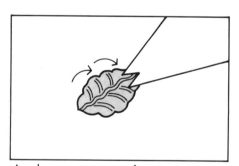

Apply even pressure during piping and move slowly, making a jerking movement gently up and down for side leaf veins.

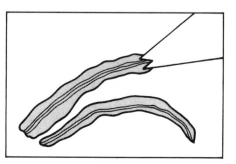

To make narrow or wider leaves, move the bag along with an even pressure. Pull the bag away for a pointed end.

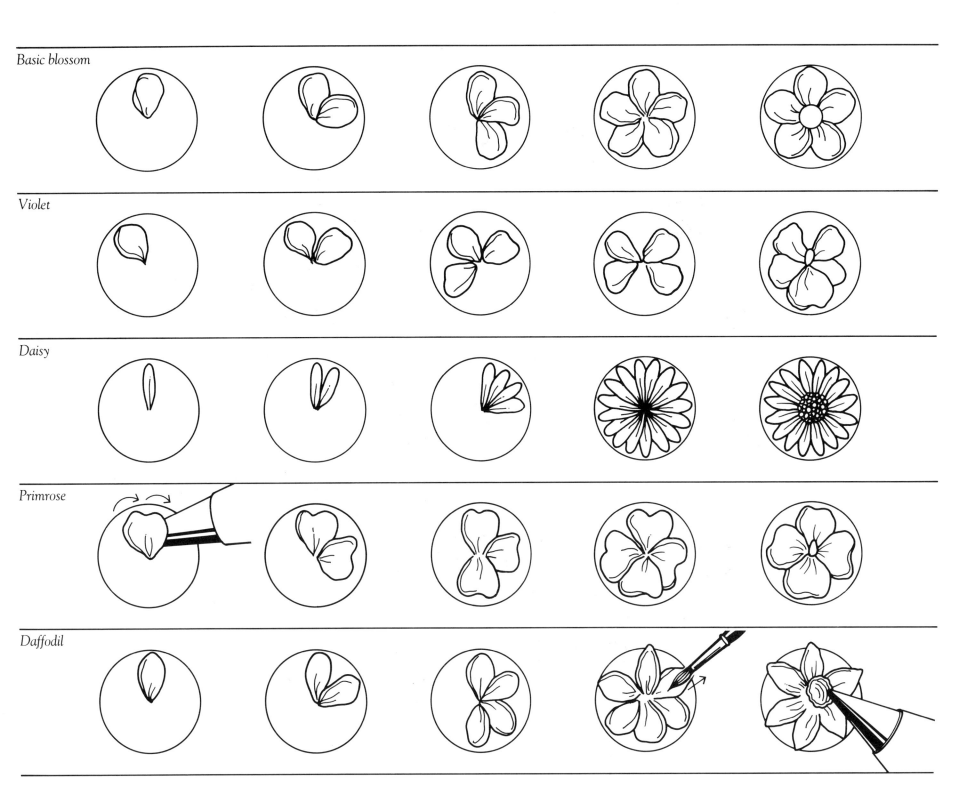

Basic blossom

Violet

Daisy

Primrose

Daffodil

BUTTERCREAM DESIGNS

Use the flowers and leaves described on the previous page to decorate your buttercream specials!
Make the flowers easier to handle by removing them from the waxed paper straight from the refrigerator.
Stems and leaves can be piped directly onto the buttercream-covered cake, if preferred.

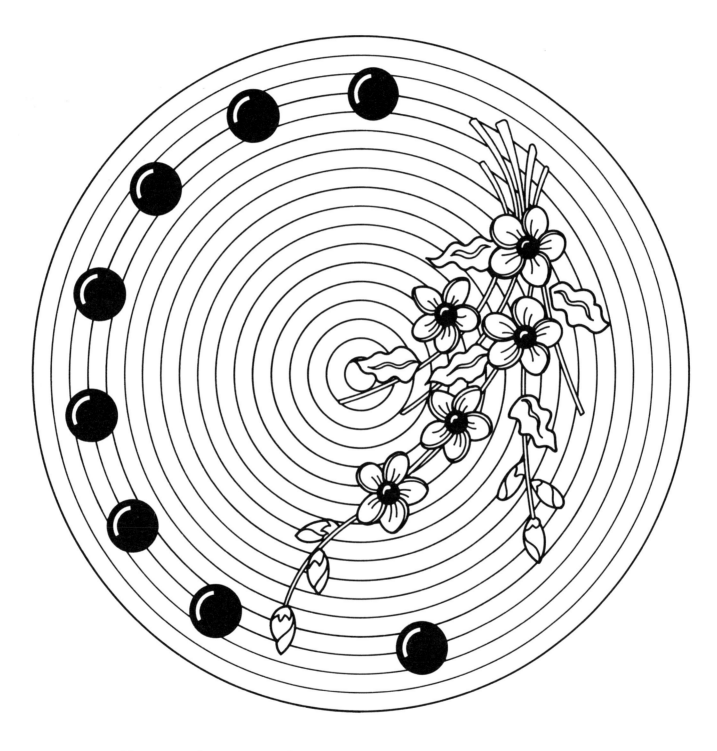

Use a serrated scraper to comb the top of a buttercream-covered cake. Decorate with
flowers, leaves and chocolate drops.

Here are 12 designs for decorating buttercream cakes. Select one design and repeat on each individual segment of your cake.

Runout Collars

Elegant runout collars as a border decoration add a spectacular extra dimension to both royal iced and sugarpaste-covered cakes. As well as full collars in various sizes for round and square cakes, patterns are given for hexagonal cakes. There are also beautiful floral collars and corner designs, each with helpful step-by-step drawings. The floral collar overlays have the added feature of a prefabricated section to create more interest and detail to the overall appearance.

To adapt this delicate modern design for beginners or to make a more solid design for a man's cake, simply omit the open sections when piping and flooding with runout icing.

A selection of decorative ideas to use in the open sections of the runout collar when it has dried.

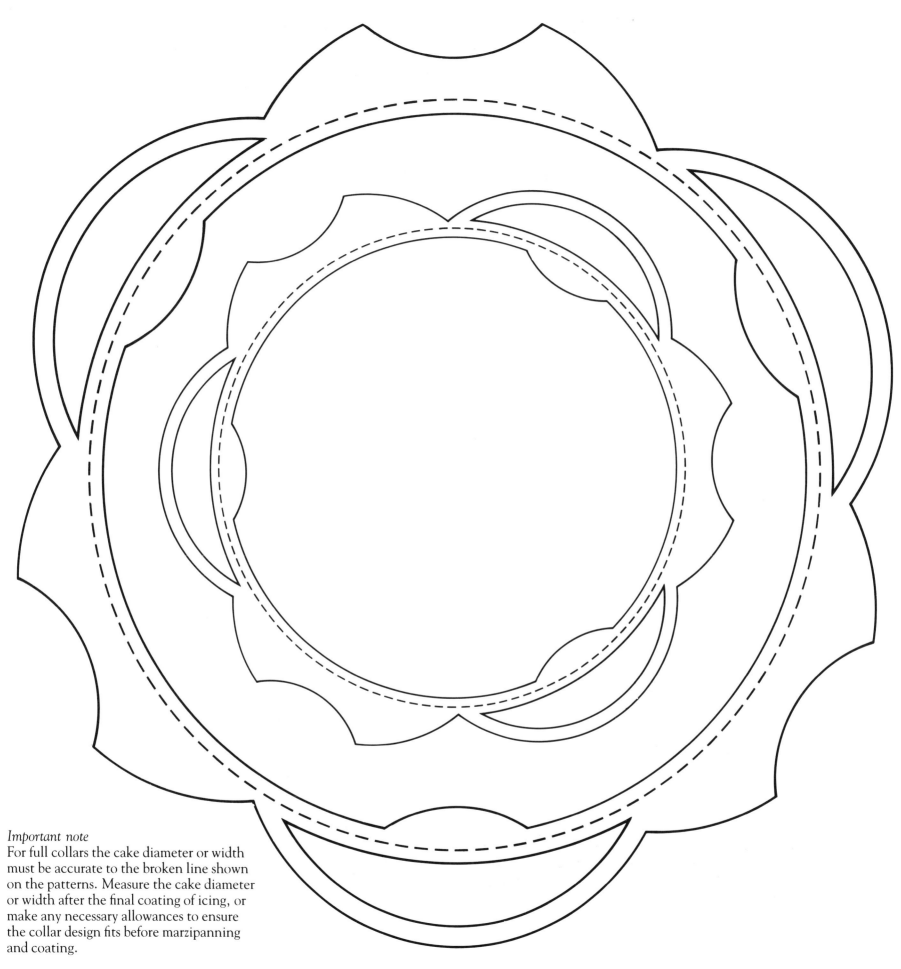

Important note
For full collars the cake diameter or width must be accurate to the broken line shown on the patterns. Measure the cake diameter or width after the final coating of icing, or make any necessary allowances to ensure the collar design fits before marzipanning and coating.

RUNOUT SIDE COLLARS

Four designs for full side collars. A corner filler or overlay can be used to conceal the joins if required; otherwise use linework to make a feature of the joins. Design D can be used as a full side collar or joined to make a full square collar. As with all runout patterns, the open sections of Designs B and D may be omitted and left solid.

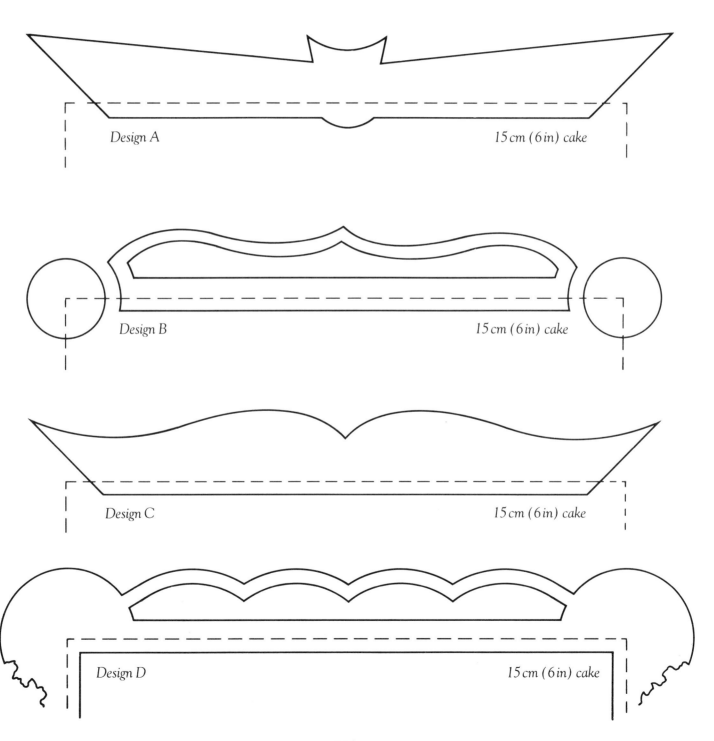

Design A   *15 cm (6 in) cake*

Design B   *15 cm (6 in) cake*

Design C   *15 cm (6 in) cake*

Design D   *15 cm (6 in) cake*

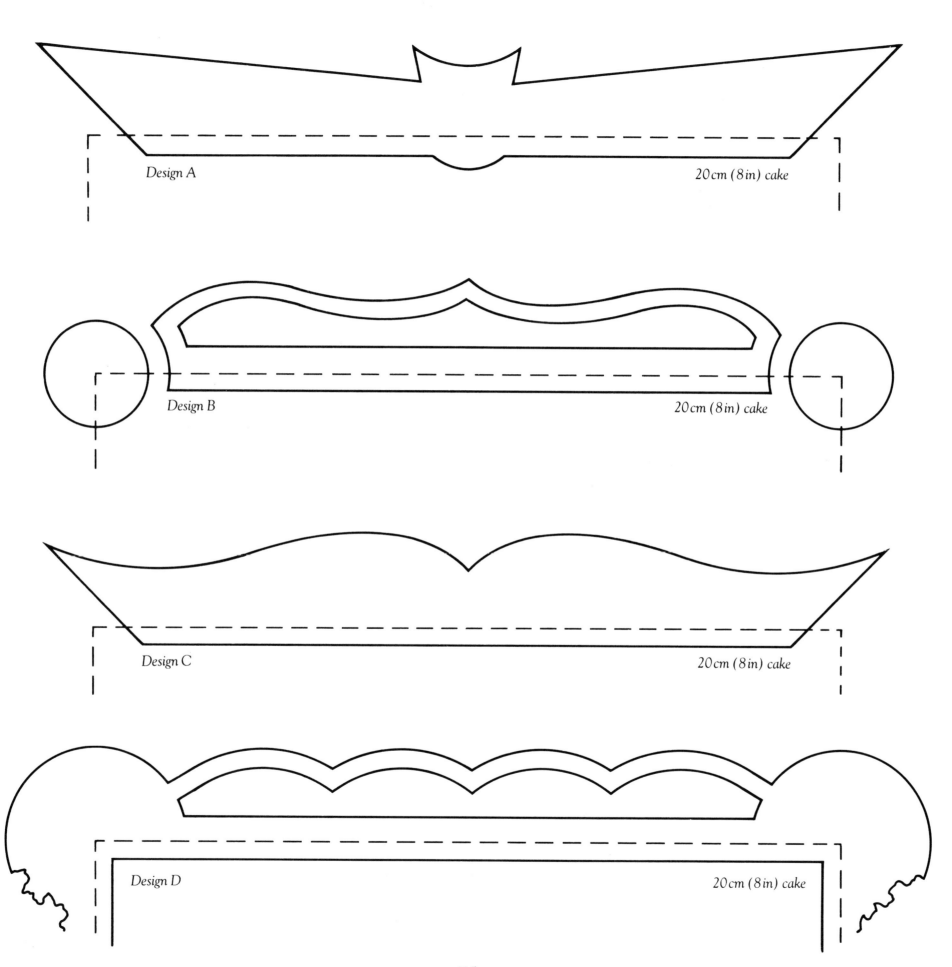

Design A   20cm (8in) cake

Design B   20cm (8in) cake

Design C   20cm (8in) cake

Design D   20cm (8in) cake

RUNOUT COLLARS FOR HEXAGONAL CAKES

Hexagonal cakes are popular for all occasions; use these sectioned collars to solve your border design problems. Hexagonal cakes are measured from point to point.

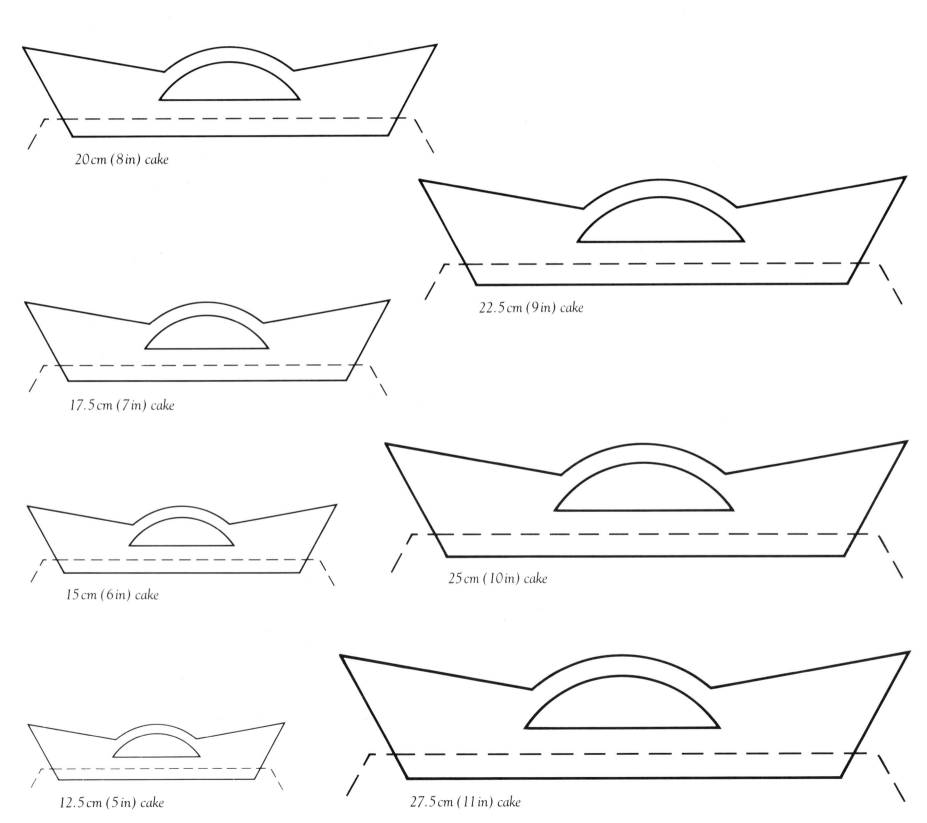

20 cm (8 in) cake

22.5 cm (9 in) cake

17.5 cm (7 in) cake

15 cm (6 in) cake

25 cm (10 in) cake

12.5 cm (5 in) cake

27.5 cm (11 in) cake

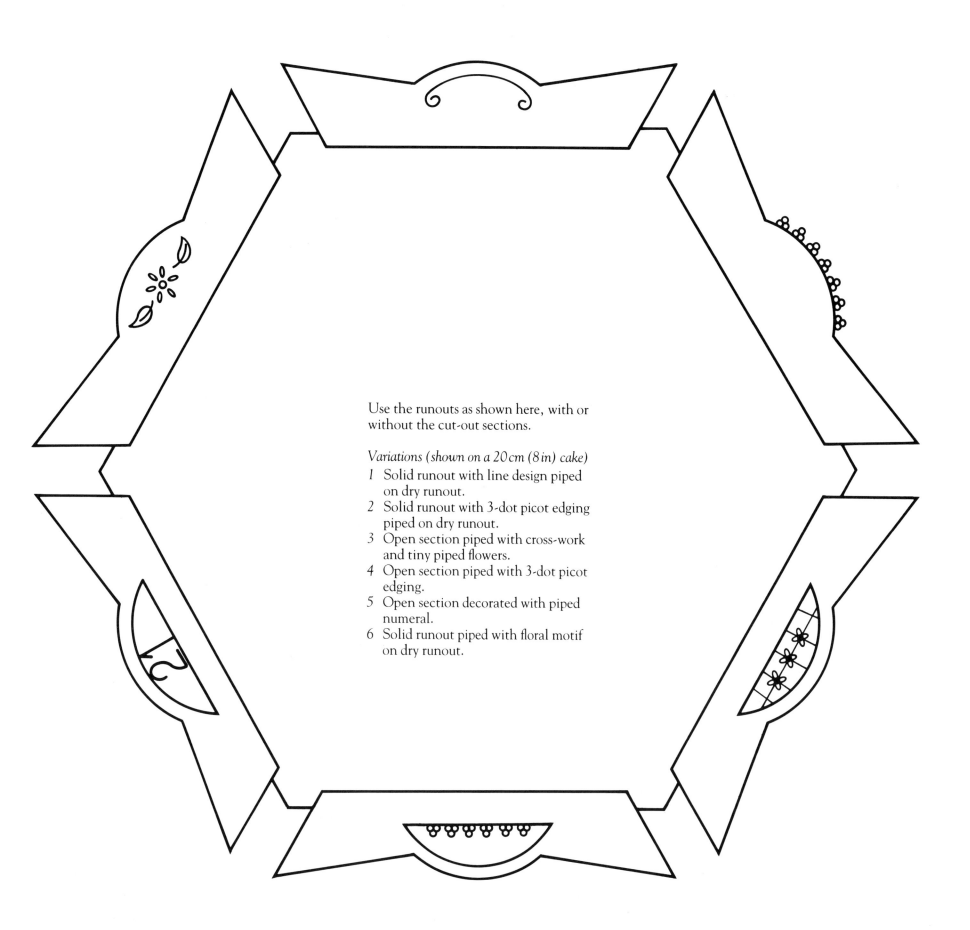

Use the runouts as shown here, with or
without the cut-out sections.

Variations (shown on a 20 cm (8 in) cake)
1 Solid runout with line design piped
   on dry runout.
2 Solid runout with 3-dot picot edging
   piped on dry runout.
3 Open section piped with cross-work
   and tiny piped flowers.
4 Open section piped with 3-dot picot
   edging.
5 Open section decorated with piped
   numeral.
6 Solid runout piped with floral motif
   on dry runout.

RUNOUT CORNER COLLARS

A runout corner collar design that is easy to pipe and quick to flood.
Once the collars are dry, you can decorate them further with flowers, bells or other suitable motifs to
complement the overall theme of your cake.

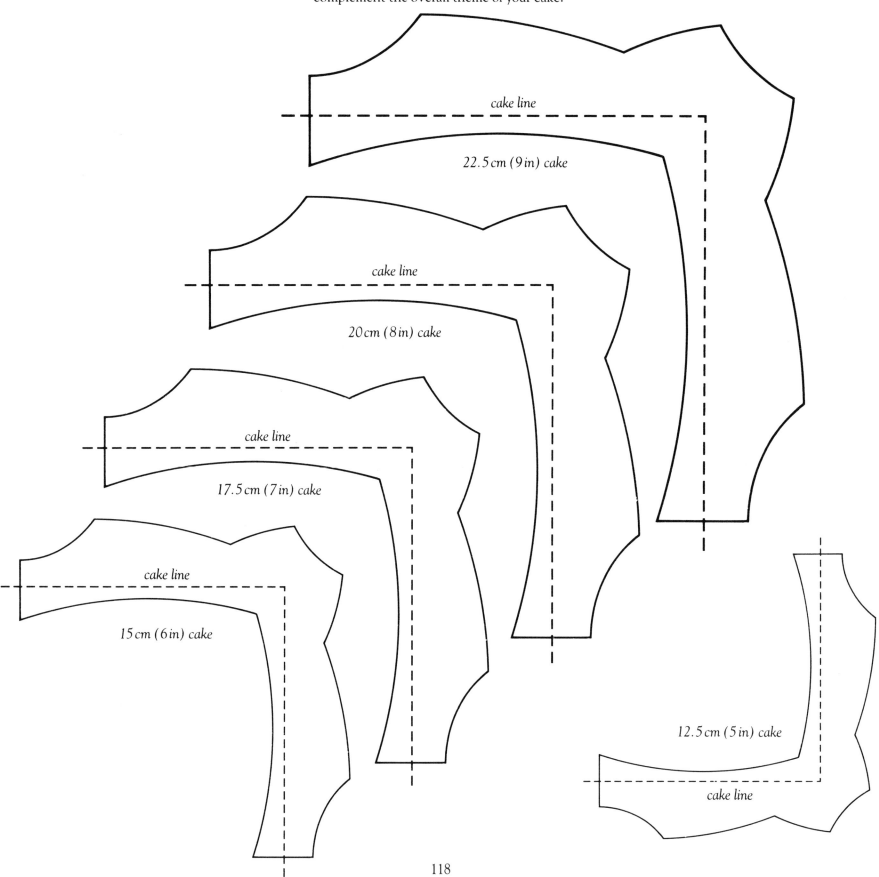

cake line

22.5 cm (9 in) cake

cake line

20 cm (8 in) cake

cake line

17.5 cm (7 in) cake

cake line

15 cm (6 in) cake

12.5 cm (5 in) cake

cake line

Floral runout collars

How to pipe a floral runout collar

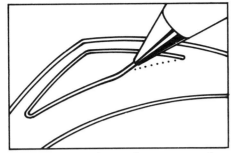

Place a piece of waxed paper over the design and outline using royal icing and a No 1 tube (tip).

Complete the piping as shown, ensuring that the floral design is then attached to the runout collar.

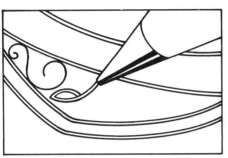

Pipe in the flower and leaf design using various coloured royal icings with fine tubes (tips).

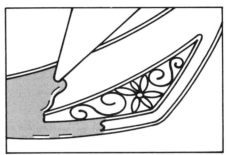

Following the piped outline, neatly flood-in using runout icing. Allow to dry, then attach to the cake with a little icing.

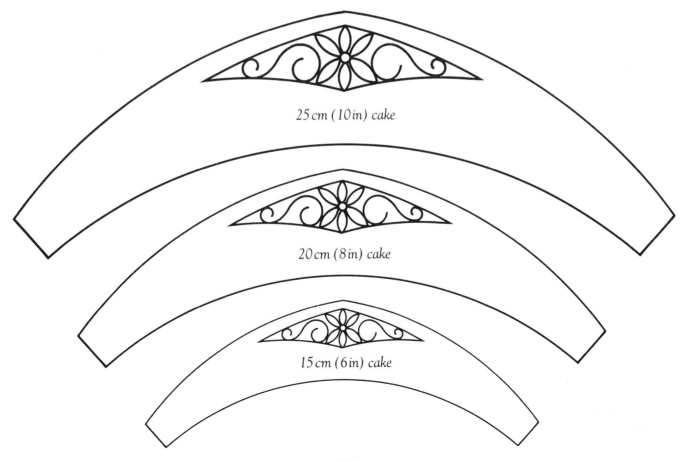

25 cm (10 in) cake

20 cm (8 in) cake

15 cm (6 in) cake

FLORAL CORNER DESIGNS

These attractive floral corner pieces have been developed by the basic runout collar technique.
The pieces are smaller than a corner collar, but made and applied to the cake in the conventional manner.
Utilize the space between the corners to introduce linework and tiny piped border work.

HOW TO MAKE A RUNOUT CORNER PIECE

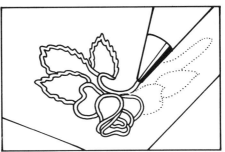

Place waxed paper over the design on the page. Outline the design using royal icing and a No 1 tube (tip).

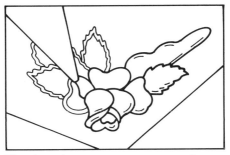

Flood-in the various sections with appropriately coloured runout icing. Allow to dry.

When dry, paint on detail, veins and shading using edible food colour and a fine paint brush.

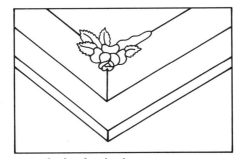

Attach the finished runout corner pieces to a sugarpaste-coated or royal-iced cake.

120

Cake line

Cake line

Cake line

Cake line

Cake line

Cake line

Cake line

Cake line

Suitable for cakes of various sizes from 15 cm (6 in) to 25 cm (10 in) depending on the amount of space required between each corner shape.

Use the space between and on the cake side to pipe linework, add ribbon or even more flowers!

FLORAL COLLAR OVERLAYS

HOW TO MAKE A COLLAR WITH FLORAL OVERLAY

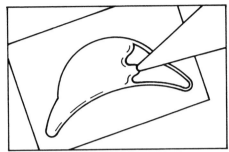

1 Outline and flood-in the collar shape using the same method as described on page 119. Allow to dry.

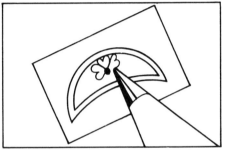

2 Make one floral overlay for each collar section using the same method given on page 119. Allow to dry.

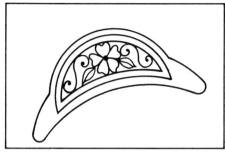

3 Remove the overlay from the waxed paper and position accurately onto the collar with royal icing.

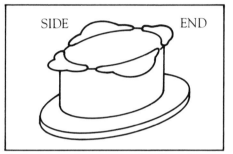

4 Remove the prepared collars from the waxed paper. Attach the two end collars and two side collars to the cake as shown.

END SECTIONS

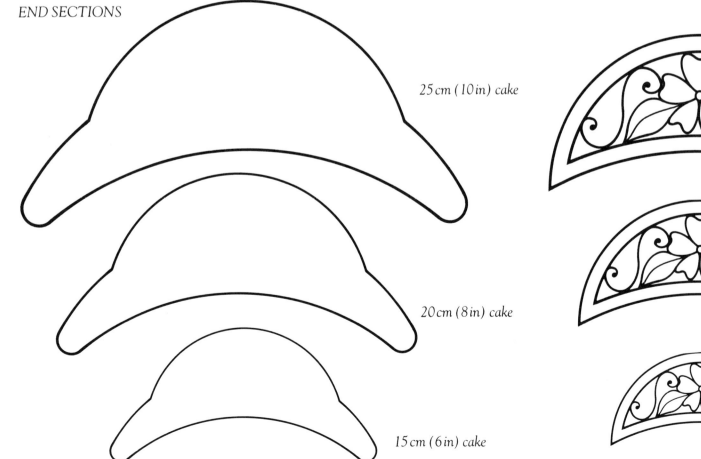

25 cm (10 in) cake

20 cm (8 in) cake

15 cm (6 in) cake

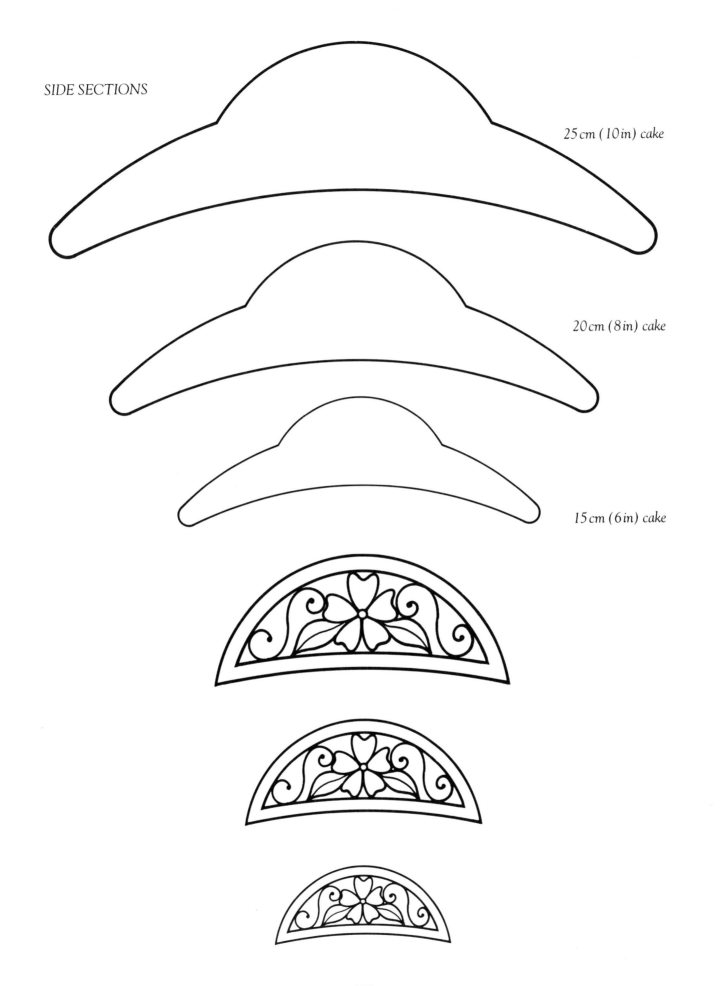

SIDE SECTIONS

25 cm (10 in) cake

20 cm (8 in) cake

15 cm (6 in) cake

CAKE SIDE AND BOARD DESIGNS

These attractive designs can be piped directly on to the cake side in appropriately coloured icing, painted on to the cake with edible food colouring, or carried out in brush embroidery. Making a template (see below) and using a cake tilter or turntable with a tilting device will make the work much easier. Instead of simply edging a cake board with ribbon or a band, board designs add further complementary decoration to a cake. Delicate lace pieces have also been included in this section.

HOW TO MAKE A CAKE SIDE TEMPLATE

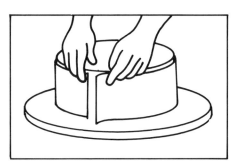

1 Wrap a strip of greaseproof (waxed) paper around the iced cake, measuring and marking where necessary.

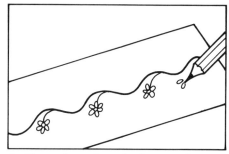

3 Trace the cake side design of your choice onto the paper directly from the page.

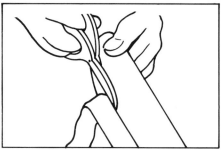

2 Cut the paper to make an accurate template the depth of the side of the cake.

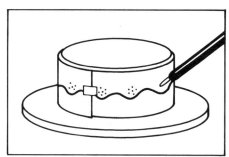

4 Secure the template to the cake side with masking tape. Pin-prick the design ready for piping or painting.

Wedding or anniversary

Autumn

12.5 cm (5 in) cake

20 cm (8 in) cake

22.5 cm (9 in) cake

SIDE DESIGN STENCILS

CAKE BOARD DESIGNS

Try coordinating the board decoration with the main theme of your design.

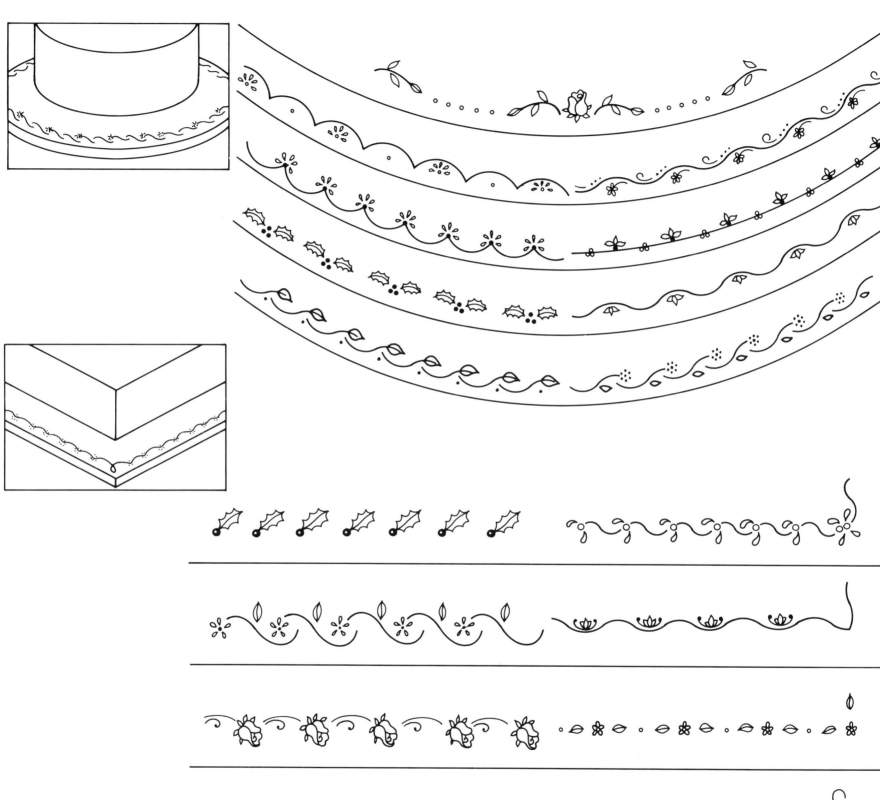

PIPED LACE PIECES

Finely piped lace pieces make the perfect decoration for any sugarpaste-covered celebration cake; they also look attractive when used on royal-iced cakes. This comprehensive selection of designs has been specially created with a floral theme in mind.

HOW TO PIPE LACE PIECES

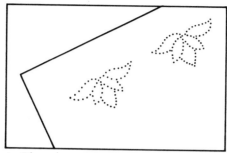

1 Place long narrow strips or small squares of waxed paper over the design of your choice.

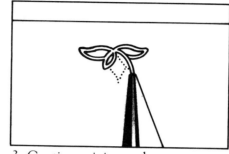

3 Continue piping as shown, building up the detail until the shape is complete. Proceed with the next piece.

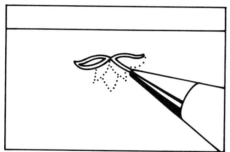

2 Commence piping, usually from the base of the lace piece, using a fine tube (tip) and fresh royal icing.

4 Complete the required number of shapes. Allow to dry, then carefully remove from the paper and attach to the cake.

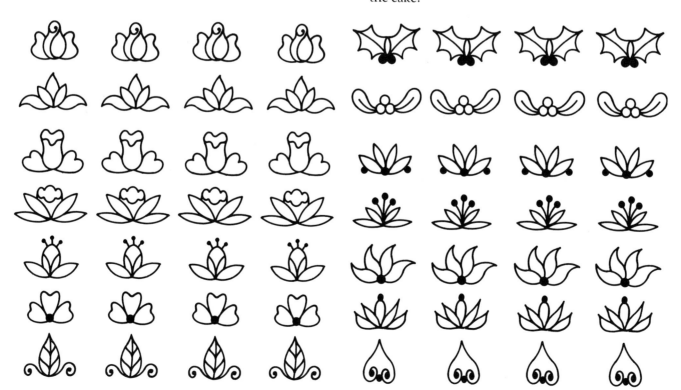

LETTERING

Here is an invaluable array of lettering styles, popular phrases, inscriptions, monograms and numbers to suit every celebration cake and novelty. Spacing is probably the most important aspect of lettering. This is fully explained, together with positioning lettering, centralizing and lettering on a curve – all to help you produce professional-looking results. The easy to follow patterns and instructions enable cake decorators of all skill levels to add the perfect wording to their sugarcraft creations. Many different sugarcraft techniques can be used for lettering, such as piping, runout and stencilling; all producing very different looking designs. A useful selection of shapes suitable for plaques has been included on which to mount monograms or a message.

USING THE PATTERNS

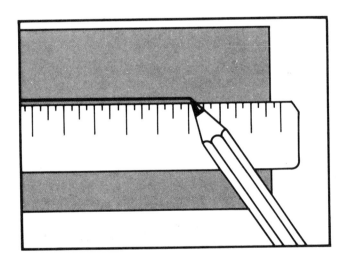

1 Using a ruler, draw a straight line on a piece of tracing paper large enough to fit your required word. Use a pair of compasses or suitable curved object if you want lettering on a curve.

2 Place the tracing paper over the lettering style of your choice, aligning the straight line with the base of the first letter in your word.

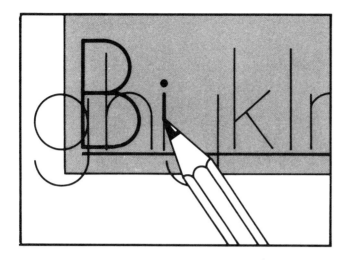

3 Carefully trace the letter, then move the tracing paper and re-align the straight line and your previously traced letter over the next letter in your word.

4 Continue as for steps 2 and 3 until you have completed your word. For a multi-worded inscription prepare each word on a separate sheet of tracing paper.

5 Place the tracings of your two or more prepared words over each other and rearrange them into a suitably balanced layout, taking into account the other decoration of your cake top shape and size to practise with first.

6 When you are satisfied with the layout of your words, attach them together with masking tape or make a new tracing of the finished layout. Place the template onto your cake top and prick through with a pointed scriber to transfer a pin-prick dotted line onto your cake ready for piping.

POINTS TO REMEMBER WHEN LETTERING

DESIGN TO YOUR OWN ABILITY TO PIPE

Do not choose a really fancy or difficult style of lettering that you may not be able to pipe. Start off with easy lettering until your piping skills improve.

SELECT LETTERING WITH THE RECIPIENT IN MIND

Select lettering to suit the style they would most appreciate on their cake, an adult would probably prefer something attractive with perhaps more detail, while the style chosen for a child is best kept simple and easy to read.

SELECT LETTERING WITH THE OCCASION IN MIND

Work with the occasion in mind whilst designing your cake, it may be a formal or fun occasion, a lively or serious event. Lettering styles can convey many different moods and themes. Take for instance the two styles of the word 'Christmas' below, the one on the left is an Old English style that would be suitable for a formal design, probably for an adult, whilst the style on the right is far more modern, lively and bold and would best be appreciated by a younger person on an informal celebration cake.

Christmas   **CHRISTMAS**

SELECT LETTERING WITH A COLOUR SCHEME IN MIND

When choosing your lettering and its subsequent colouring, try to match or contrast with a scheme already apparent such as the bridesmaid's dress colour, table settings, house colours or logo.
Remember too, when adding lettering to torten or gâteaux, that if a flavour is being used an appropriately coloured inscription would help carry the theme through and make it easier for the recipient to decide what the cake should taste of.

SPACING

Spacing is probably the most important aspect of lettering, even the best drawn and balanced letters forming a word can look entirely disjointed if the spacing is not correct. The rule is not to space the letters equally, but to space them to appear with equal intervals between each letter. Fig 1 below shows a word with equal spacing between letters, Fig 2 shows the same word with the spacing correctly used to give an effect of an equal interval of space between each letter thus creating a pleasing continuity to the word.

It is because of the shape of the letters such as L, A, T, V, C that we must allow more space around them than most other letters of the alphabet, so when using these, very little extra space between them is required. Having said this, many of the modern lettering styles in this book will require spacing again, but you will soon become accustomed to achieving a good visual balance and pleasing arrangement.

Fig 1   *Fig 2*

CENTRALIZING

To centralize a curved or even straight word on a cake, do not rely on the often recommended method of dividing the number of letters in the word equally in half as problems can occur. For instance, in the word 'Birthday' below which contains eight letters, dividing the word in half would result in the right-hand side being wider than the left, this is due to the fact that the three wide and one thin letter on the left-hand side do not occupy as much space as the four wide letters on the the right-hand side of the word.

Incorrect Centralizing by dividing in half the number of letters within the word.

Correct Centralizing by dividing in half the measured length of the word.

POSITIONING

When you become more confident with your piping skills and techniques you will no doubt want to pipe directly onto your cake, and you will find suitable styles for this method in this section. To position the words use narrow strips of thin card, plastic or clean wood to give the required spacing for the height of your letters as in Fig 3 or for slanted letters as in Fig 5. Another method is to make a thin card mask of the outline of a word, cut out the area where the word will be piped and place the mask onto the cake top ready to pipe on the letters.

Remember – until you have complete confidence in your ability to write onto a cake with coloured icing, pipe the words in the same colour as the base icing or sugarpaste then if you make a mistake you can lift off the icing with a paint brush without leaving marks on the cake top, as would be the case had you used a dark brown or bright red! Once you are happy with your piped lettering, overpipe with a coloured icing.

Fig 3   *Fig 4*   *Fig 5*

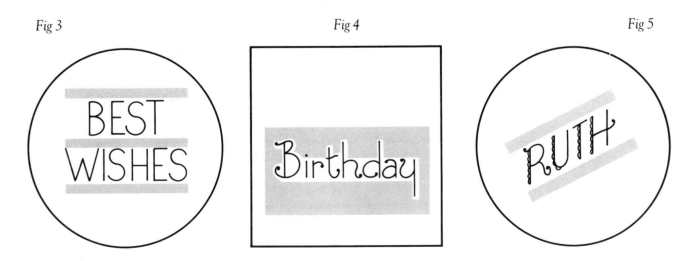

LETTERING ON A CURVE

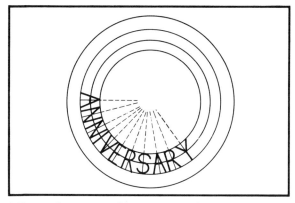

1 Draw the required lettering as described on page 131 using an accurate drawing of a circle the size you require – don't forget to allow for the border on your cake. Notice how the vertical centres of each letter radiate from the centre point of the circle (shown by the dotted line) to achieve a balanced appearance.

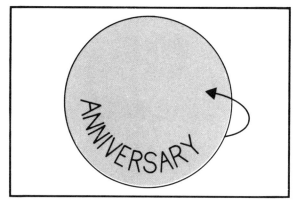

2 Make a tracing of the word onto a circle of tracing or greaseproof (waxed) paper.

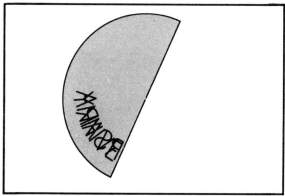

3 Fold the tracing in half through the middle of the word using the top outward facing corners of the letters (or letter area) as opposites.

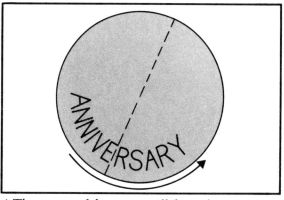

4 The crease of the paper will form the centre line for the inscription.

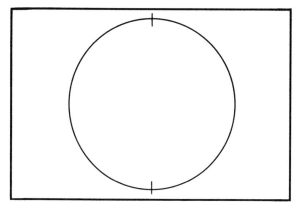

5 Mark a centre (in this case a vertical line) on the cake top.

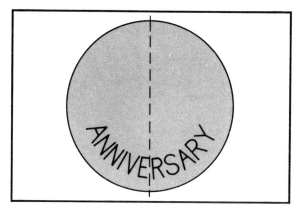

6 Align the crease on the paper template with the centre line on the cake and then pin-prick the word onto the cake top using the method described in Step 6 on page 131.

1 A lettering style can be used for more than one sugarcraft technique as shown in these illustrations. Here we see basic single stroke, directly piped lettering using a No 1 or No 2 tube (tip).

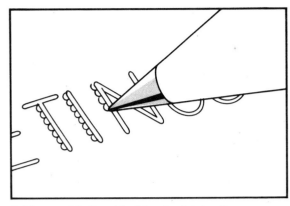

2 Using a No 0 or No 00 tube (tip) a fine scalloped decoration can be introduced at the side of each letter to add extra colour and interest.

3 Basic lettering can be overpiped with coloured icing either fully or partly as shown here on the bottom half only of each letter. Red lettering overpiped on the top half with white icing looks nice for Christmas cakes.

4 Using the same template with a wider tube (tip), say a No 3 or No 4, and royal icing. Alternatively, use the wide tubes with buttercream; pipe the letters onto waxed paper, place in the refrigerator to firm and then peel off as required to decorate your gâteaux, novelties and cheesecakes.

5 Pipe the letters using a No 2 tube (tip) and add a serif to enhance the style a little more. This type of letter can be directly piped onto the cake or made on waxed paper and attached to the cake when dry. This will save mistakes on the actual cake, but do make a few spares as they are rather fragile!

6 Using the method described in Step 5, make prepared letters and then colour one half of each letter with edible petal dusting powder, or use an airbrush to spray on edible liquid food colouring.

A B C D E F G H I
J K L M N O P Q R
S T U V W X Y Z

a b c d e f g h i j k
l m n o p q r s t
u v w x y z

To create a more distinctive effect with a basic lettering style, add embellishments to the final letter, as shown.

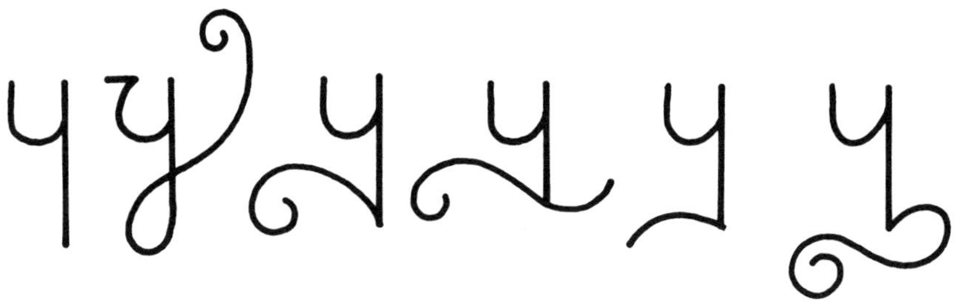

Embellishments can also be added to the first or capital letter of a name or inscription, as shown.

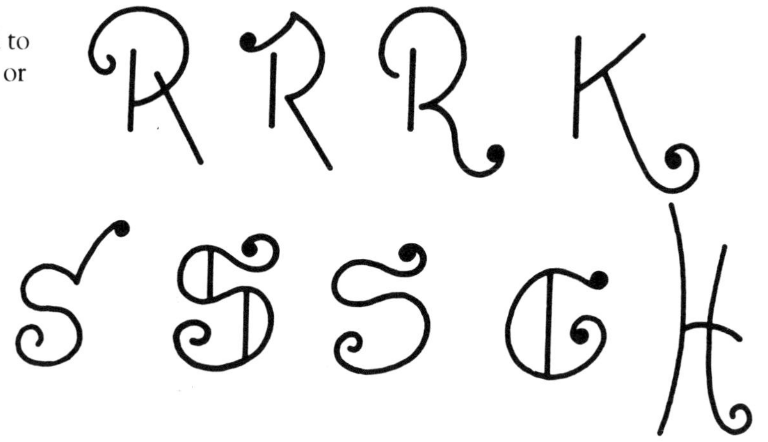

R R R K

y y y y y y y

S S S G

Embellished Basic Lettering

A B C D E F G H
I J K L M N O P Q
R S T U V W X Y Z

Direct Piping Style NO1

A B C D E F G H I J K L M
N O P P Q Q R R S T T U U
W X Y Z Z

a b c d e f g h i j k l m n
o p q r s t u v w x y z

DIRECT PIPING STYLE NO2

This curvy lettering is very easy to pipe as the majority of the letters are piped in one complete operation.

ABCDEFGHIJKLMN
OPQRSTUVWXYZ

a b c d e f g h i j k l m n
o p q r s t u v w x y z

SCRIPT STYLE NO1

A modern script style based on oval shapes.

ABCDEFGHIJKLM
NOPQRSTUVWXYZ
1234567890

SCRIPT STYLE NO2

A traditional script lettering, this classic style is always in use for directly piped inscriptions.

ABCDEFGHIJKL
MNOPQRSTUV
WXYZ

abcdefghijklmno
pqrstuvwxyz

Thankyou   Christening

CUT-OUT STYLE

A bold lettering based on geometric shapes that is ideal for children's cakes.
Cut out the shapes using a sharp knife, rules and a selection of food cutters. Try texturing the paste before
cutting with a ribbed rolling pin.

ABCDEFGHIJ

KLMNOPQRS

TUVWXYZ

123456789

BIRTHDAY

Floral lettering

Use this delicately adorned lettering with floral embellishments to complement other floral decoration
on your cake.

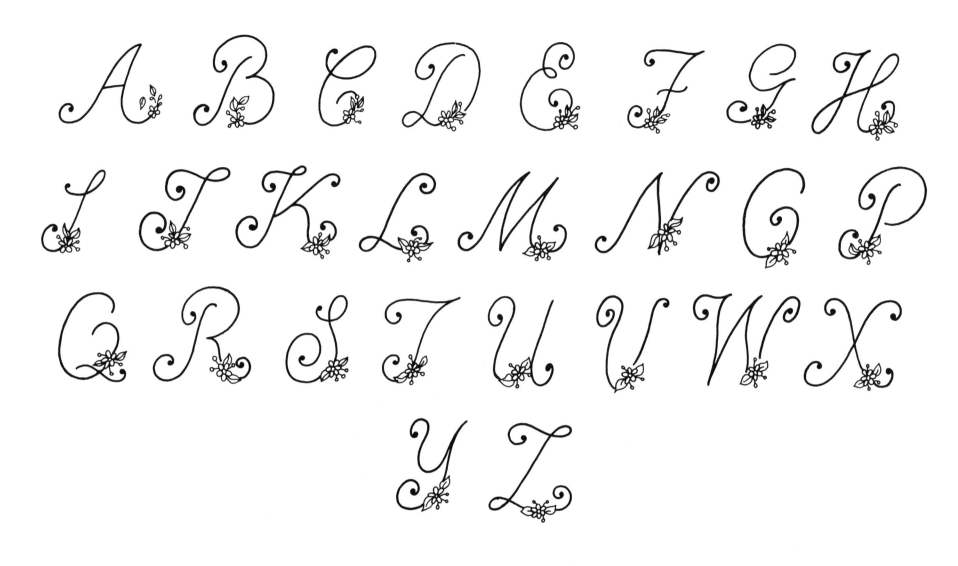

Direct piping style no3

ABCDEFG
HIJKLMNO
PQRSTUVW
XYZ

Runout style no1

A bold, simple outline particularly useful for children's cakes. This style can be runout, painted, cut-out from sugarpaste or simply outlined and filled with icing or piping jelly.

ABCDEFGH IJ
KLMNOPQRS
TUVWXYZ

Script Style No3

A modern script style with beautifully curving capital letters. This dainty and delicate style is suitable for many different cake tops and confectionery.

A B C D E F G
H I J K L M N
O P Q R S T U
V W X Y Z

A B C D E F G H I J
K L M N O P Q R
S T U V W X Y Z

a b c d e f g h i j k l m n o p
q r s t u v w x y z

FUN LETTERING

Use this style of lettering for any informal type cake. You can either prepare the letters singly, or make a runout plaque with all the letters attached as in the 'Seasons Greetings' and 'Easter'.

ABCDEFGH
IJKLMNO
PQRSTUV
WXYZ

HAPPY NEW YEAR

NOUGAT

HAPPY BIRTHDAY

JASON

MERRY CHRISTMAS

This easy-to-space lettering can be executed using a variety of techniques making it useful for different applications.

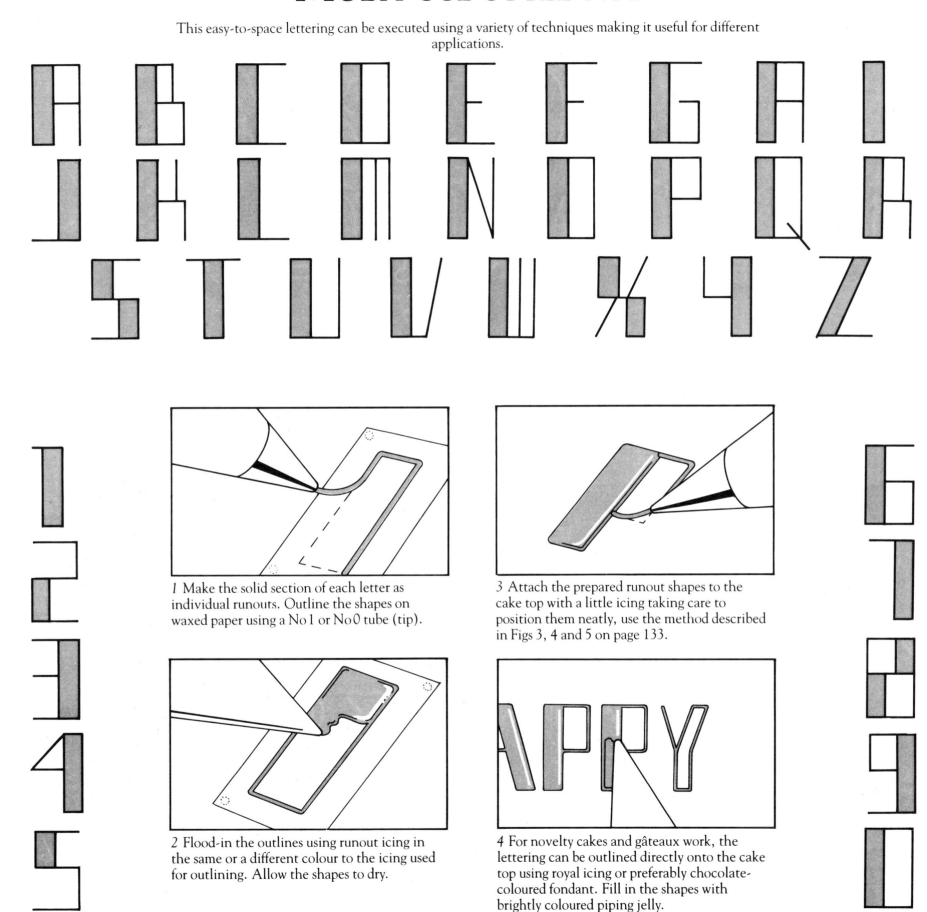

1 Make the solid section of each letter as individual runouts. Outline the shapes on waxed paper using a No 1 or No 0 tube (tip).

2 Flood-in the outlines using runout icing in the same or a different colour to the icing used for outlining. Allow the shapes to dry.

3 Attach the prepared runout shapes to the cake top with a little icing taking care to position them neatly, use the method described in Figs 3, 4 and 5 on page 133.

4 For novelty cakes and gâteaux work, the lettering can be outlined directly onto the cake top using royal icing or preferably chocolate-coloured fondant. Fill in the shapes with brightly coloured piping jelly.

A selection of popular inscriptions and phrases to complete your cake design and decoration.

Ruby

Silver

Golden

Wedding

Best WISHES

HAPPY EASTER

Greetings

Best Wishes

Engagement

Christening

Mother

Congratulations

Retirement

Hello!

Anniversary

Happy
Birthday

Happy
Birthday

Happy
Birthday

Happy
Birthday

Happy
Birthday

Happy
Birthday

HAPPY
BIRTHDAY

HAPPY BIRTHDAY

Congratulations

Best Wishes

Easter

Happy Birthday

Merry Christmas

LETTERING WITH MOTIF

These useful stencils combine a decorative motif within the design.

Designing Monograms

This monogram alphabet retains the traditional character of Lombardic lettering but with a simplified appearance for modern use.

1 Make individual tracings of the letters required for your monogram.

2 Overlap the tracings as shown.

3 Arrange the letters to create a balanced effect.

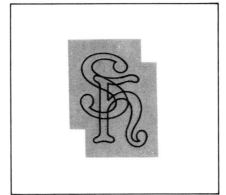

4 Re-trace the arranged monogram onto paper as a single template.

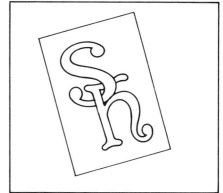

5 The runout monogram mounted on a plaque (see page 160 for plaque shapes).

Variations
Outline letters either using one colour, or a different colour for each letter.
Fill-in with runout icing, again in one colour, for both letters or two different colours, one for each letter.
Allow the first flooded letter to dry before filling the second.
Use edible gold or silver colour to paint the monogram when dry.
Before filling in with coloured icing, such as blue or pink for the letters, colour the piped, dry outline with gold or silver food colour for an attractive edging.

For use on multi-tiered cakes, the monogram alphabet is provided here in three graduated sizes.

ABCDEFGHIJ
KLMNOPQRSTU
VWXYZ

ABCDEFGHIJ
KLMNOPQRSTU
VWXYZ

Numerals

Numerals can be piped directly on to cake tops in various edible mediums, or made as runouts and attached to a runout plaque upright.

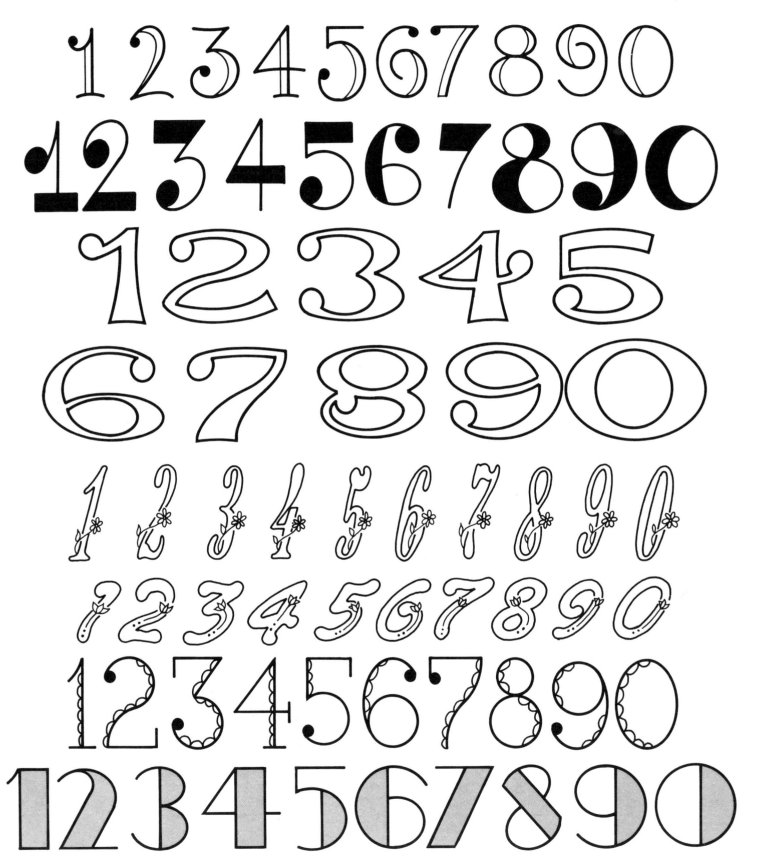

SHAPES

You will be surprised at how many times a cake design involves one of these shapes.

PLAQUE SHAPES

A useful selection of shapes suitable for plaques on which to mount your monograms, greetings, flowers or other designs. Make them as runouts or cut the shapes from thinly rolled sugarpaste.